Mindfully Unraveling

Body Awareness as I Slip Away

Mindfully Unraveling

Body Awareness as I Slip Away

RHONDA PATZIA

ISBN: 978-0-9858077-8-8

Published and printed in the United States of America by the Write Place. Cover design by Mathew R. Kelly. Interior design by Alexis Thomas, the Write Place. For more information, please contact:

the Write Place
709 Main Street, Suite 2
Pella, Iowa 50219
www.thewriteplace.biz

CIRCLE OF WOMEN LOGO
Mathew R. Kelly

CHILD OF THE WIND
Written by Bruce Cockburn
Used by permission of Rotten Kiddies Music, LLC c/o Carlin America, Inc.

The text size in this book was selected by the author to make it accessible to the visually impaired.

Open me carefully . . .

**emily dickinson, written on
the envelope of a letter to her
sister-in-law**

CONTENTS

Introduction: Body Awareness as I Slip Away

I. Writing: Awareness Through the Written Word

II. Body to Body: Connecting with Women

III. Bodies in Focus: A Photography Project of Seeing Women

. . . who though she was
desperately ill nevertheless
claimed the right to live
with full intensity.

susan griffin, "what her body thought"

Sand Dream

I'm swinging. I'm on a child's swing that isn't attached to the ground in any way. I'm moving through empty sky, back and forth and back and forth, higher and higher. The day is sunny and clear with only a few fluffy white clouds here and there. The ground is far below. I'm happy and carefree.

With a sudden flash of dream confusion my swing breaks, and I crash to the earth hard. I feel the ground through my body and, still doubled over, I struggle to my feet. A concerned friend is at my side, asking if I am hurt.

"No," I answer quickly. "Look, not a scratch." I don't have a scratch, because I am covered head-to-toe with winter clothing: coat with a fringed hood, gloves, snow pants. But then I realize I'm not okay. "I really hurt inside," I say.

I try to dust off the dirt from the fall, but sand begins to pour from my clothes. I get some on my friend, and she says something like "Watch it!" and leaves quickly. I feel depressed. I begin walking. I forget how much I hurt because I'm upset at the grainy nuisance that won't stop. Soon my frustration is replaced by curiosity. When I reach my front porch, the sand mesmerizes me as it falls from my body with more and more momentum. I take off my winter gear, rest in the sun, and consider the pile it makes.

Like a movie close-up, my eyes zoom in on the sand. The image blurs, and I wake.

Dream Meditation and More

The dream is a wonderfully accurate metaphor for my journey of living with multiple sclerosis (MS).

The Crash

In my dream, I swing euphorically in the clouds, removed and literally ungrounded. I feel happy in my dissociated state. My dream crash is surprising and sudden.

On December 24, 1996, I was at a busy shopping mall in Northern California when my vision went double. It returned to normal within a couple of days, but in April 1997, after an MRI, a lumbar puncture, and general poking and prodding around my body, a neurologist declared me diseased. I knew so little about multiple sclerosis that I wondered if it would kill me soon. I felt that I had just crashed to the ground *hard*.

It didn't seem fair! At the time of diagnosis, I was such a vigorous, healthy body, and I loved to feel how much I could do. I ran mountain trails; I cross-country skied by moonlight; I backpacked through desert canyons, up 14,000-foot peaks and around the world. When my doctor called me with a final diagnosis, I was in the darkroom. I slid to a sitting position on the floor—knees in my face—and remained still for about an hour. The light was red and the fan hummed.

Before the MS crash, how had I floated above the reality of my body? How was I metaphorically swinging in the clouds? I was psychologically removed from reality—ungrounded—because I didn't live as an integrated body, didn't acknowledge or respect my entire body. I thought I was successful, but success for me depended on dictator-like control of the rest of my body. My misguided ego made me "successfully" anorexic, "successfully" asexual, "successfully" "spiritual," and smart and talented by conventional measures. Success, I thought then, had nothing to do with *feeling* my whole body.

Disease surprised me just as the broken swing did in my dream. Both interrupted my numb euphoria, sending me plummeting to the hard ground, to base reality. Even though I had protected myself head-to-toe with winter clothing in my dream—and in real life with diet, exercise, and measurable successes—in my comfortable ungroundedness, I wasn't immune to falls. I hit base reality *hard.*

Pain

In the dream I make the dissociated claim, "Not a scratch." My first reaction to a diagnosis of MS was similar: general denial that disease would affect my life much. After all, nothing had really changed. I could still run. I could still throw a football with my husband Mike. I could still photograph and continue to pursue a career in photography. Having a disease wasn't such a bother, since I didn't really feel any physical pain from it.

After the initial denial of pain, in the dream I realize that I really hurt inside. At the time of diagnosis, even though I was still psychologically numb, or ungrounded, my entire body wasn't going to let this zombie state last. Even though I looked perfectly healthy on the outside (to the extent that people were dumbfounded that I had any health problem), MS painfully affected every move I made. When my eyesight dipped to 20/400, my photography business folded, I couldn't drive, and I couldn't read. As fatigue began to creep through my body, I didn't have energy for hikes with friends. Even though I still didn't show a scratch physically, I was really hurting inside.

Irritation

The dream sand irritates me at first. It gets in the way. The sand in some sense represents the effect of multiple sclerosis on my body. Whether the sand represents my body crumbling to dust as MS disintegrates it at an accelerated rate or the energy that disease seems to drain from me without relief, both decay and energy depletion are my reality.

I finally admitted that multiple sclerosis was changing my life. Not able to see my feet, I had to cut my toenails by feel! Generally dizzied, I negotiated most everything *by feel.* My reaction to this honesty was not just irritation with my body. I hated it intensely.

It was getting in the way of my life, I thought. I tried and tried to shake off disease, to pretend it wasn't there, just as I had worked to brush away the sand in the dream.

Although the sand bothers me only for a dream instant, estrangement from and hate of my diseased body went on for several years. I couldn't rise above my body to live happily unconnected like before. I was desperately irritated.

Awareness

After I struggle for a while against the pouring sand, a new attention to it takes me through the rest of the dream. I begin to watch it fall from me. Instead of flinging grains away angrily, I follow them as they slip from my body into a pile. My consideration of the sand is so acute that my dream ends with a close-up of it.

As my body is disintegrating from multiple sclerosis, and energy pours from me rapidly, can I be aware of my body as it goes, or comes apart, with the same meditative dream attention?

In answering this, I'm at risk here of idealizing the benefits of suffering. Let me make myself perfectly clear: pain sucks. Lameness sucks. Visual impairment sucks. It sucks that my legs cramp into knots. Not driving sucks. Not running and cross-country skiing sucks. A lack of vocational security sucks. Not knowing if I can walk tomorrow sucks. Taking awareness of my mortality into my thirties sucks. Dragging disease with me into my new marriage was a great sadness.

In light of this pain, why, then, is awareness of my body ("body" understood here as my whole self) important to my well-being at all? In my waking life, is the pain of groundedness, of feeling my diseased body, preferable to my prior dissociated existence?

Yes. Simply put, I live more freely and fully when I am aware. By feeling, really feeling, my body in time and space, I am more genuinely compassionate and peace-seeking, assertive and intentional, passionate, and visionary.

Compassionate and peace-seeking: Acute attention to my body engenders self-respect and self-love. When I didn't acknowledge my entire body/self as my identity, I struggled with self-hate, and I was more prone to compare myself to and subconsciously compete with others. With self-awareness, I'm naturally more actively loving of myself and of other people. I value all bodies. When seen as a lack of respect for bodies, war, sadly, becomes a global projection of body-hate run amok.

Assertive and intentional: When I'm aware of my body, I'm realistic about what I want to do and what I can do. With a strong and resolute voice, as well as with forthright, unyielding resolve, I'm assertive and intentional, but not because I'm pressured by society toward body-betraying successes.

Passionate: Body awareness charges me with energy. Passion that results from acute awareness of my entire self engaged in living moves me with power and integrity. With passion, all movement is adventure.

Visionary: I don't mean "visionary" as seeing things that aren't visible. Instead I mean "visionary" as seeing perceptively. A knowledge of myself as a living body gives me vision for how I connect with the world, enabling me to see possibilities for my present and future. I know where to go and where not to go, what to embrace and what to reject.

Referring to her mastectomy, Audre Lorde writes in *The Cancer Journals* about the importance of brave body awareness for living well: "For as we open ourselves more and more to the genuine conditions of our lives, women become less and less willing to tolerate those conditions unaltered, or to passively accept external and destructive controls over our lives and our identities."

Even though mindfully considering my body might necessitate feeling emotional and physical pain, I would rather suffer (to a degree, of course) than swing in the clouds, than live comfortably aloof.

Awareness is real. Awareness is intense. I'm happier when I'm so vibrantly present.

This Book
This book testifies to my personal efforts at body awareness. I began writing *Mindfully Unraveling: Body Awareness as I Slip Away* when a progressive form of multiple sclerosis

significantly weakened me. My work is a body-seeing and body-honoring response to a toxic philosophy that I had internalized.

"Don't worry. You're not your body, anyway." Such were the well-meaning but body-disregarding words of "comfort" too easily offered when I was first diagnosed with MS. The hope was to assure us all that the pained fleshy part of me was "not so important" compared to the *more real* yet intangible spirit, or soul. If my body had nothing to do with my real self, why, I thought, can't I overcome or control it and its influence?

And so after I agonized for several years at being unable to rise above my disintegrating body to live in the abstract "reality" of "pure spirit," I began the transformative work of body awareness. Since multiple sclerosis affected every corner of my being, physical and psychic, I was compelled to honestly and sometimes painfully confront my identity as a body. I learned that if I denied any aspect of my greater body—my whole self—however painful the attention, I would live weakly. With body awareness I am more powerfully and undeniably present in my life.

With my own radical presence, the world transforms, becoming clearer, becoming more and more my true home, if only for a little while. I'm alive, and I know it.

As a result of this written exploration, I lovingly and thankfully accepted that my body is my identity: I am female, a sexual being, a mother, a thinker, an artist, a feeler, a product of experience and memory, and I am ill. In *Mindfully Unraveling: Body Awareness as I Slip Away,* with disease as a backdrop, I explore these identities and more by creating a mosaic of written pieces that together demonstrate the arduous and mindful work of rooting myself in my fullest, most earthly identity.

I address five recent body attentions of mine: I practice attention through writing; I intentionally work to release desperate and frenetic ego control, valuing my body's wisdom and abandon; I face my illness boldly and directly; I explore my kinship with women; and, as a means for reconnecting with my vocation as a photographer while expressing my new vision, I respectfully exhibit together portraits of female friends and acquaintances—most of whom are naked.

The written pieces are not arranged in a specifically linear fashion, as acceptance itself continues to be a tortuous journey. But I do begin the book with a journal entry that expresses body/self hate and end with a piece on choosing motherhood as a result of body acceptance. The pieces are eclectic in content, form, and tone, some not even touching directly on my experience with disease. But together they express many of my silences—topics and stories never spoken—and embrace my past and present body, my aging and decaying body. And because life is a continuum, I won't pass away when I die.

Many of the quotations and thoughts are from Audre Lorde, my model for living intensely before dying. As she suggests, honest confrontation of the real conditions of my life, inseparable from my entire self, makes the fear weaker and the living lighter. Even though my health is out of control, as I look closely at my complex and fleeting body, I am stronger. With a smile and a shrug I tenderly recognize all experience as my life.

With body awareness my voice strengthens and lights a new and truer path. Originally I had called this book *Playing With Light,* as I use many images of light, believing it to be an appropriate metaphor for living.

Please hear my words and walk with me for a little while . . . before you explore your own life, your own silences.

I

WRITING
Awareness Through the Written Word

. . . together, here, we
will pray language. Let
us begin. Let us pray in
required sunlight.

frances driscoll, ***the rape poems***

AWARENESS THROUGH THE WRITTEN WORD
Introduction to My Writing

Every pen and keyboard stroke that made this book demonstrates how important the discipline of writing has been to me in my quest for greater awareness of myself as a body. Writing is the thread that connects all fields of study, and I have been attentive to each largely through this medium.

The process of living more fully has required grounding myself—knowing/feeling myself as a body. Among other attentions, this grounding demands mindful, intellectual, emotional, and semantic work in order to dismantle some of the old, body-debilitating "givens" that negatively affect my feelings, thoughts, and actions.

I believe the division of mind and body that much of philosophy and theology has constructed is a metaphysical presupposition with radical consequences. This split leaves many humans fragmented and weak. Mindfully living beyond this largely accepted "truth" has required from me superhuman, or rather uniquely human, self-discipline. The phrase "living beyond" is really inaccurate because it suggests that truer and fuller life necessitates occupying a space "out there," apart, ungrounded. For me to say that I "live beyond" body-hurtful philosophy and language really means that I will live, aware of the full reality of my life.

How has the discipline of writing aided and complemented my body awareness work, my aim of grounding myself? Succinctly, I am more in touch with my total, integrated self because I write, experimenting with different genres. In this section, I wrote my thoughts in response to published writers; I wrote my ideas and feelings in general; I closely considered my dreams; I experimented with freewriting; and I wrote of my body both in the distant and nearer past. Through writing, I consider what I think and feel, what I sense and imagine, where and how I go. Attention to myself through writing has been revelatory and intense. Groundedness begets strong and confident sure-footedness.

Integrating the many pieces I have written into this meaningful book was a further step toward using writing for body awareness. Consideration of both the parts and the whole encourages and parallels attention to myself as a body. Neither my body nor this book is a patchwork of unrelated pieces. I hope the whole work hangs together like a body mosaic—a beautiful one!

JOURNAL WRITING

I began keeping journals when I was twelve. My first was called a diary, and it locked, which taught me that personal expression must be something sacred—maybe dangerous. The discipline of journal writing makes me acutely aware of my body's movement through space and encourages me to keep moving.

Since that young age, I never stopped exploring the world through journal writing until I was diagnosed with MS. As my words stopped, my body became more alien to me: in my present I ceased tracing my thoughts and feelings, as well as my physical passions and pursuits. Consequently, I had no imagination for the future. I was powerless.

I found my words again, beginning with the journal exercise below. James W. Pennebaker, psychologist and researcher into the health benefits of personal writing, suggests as an insightful and transformational exercise, writing for four consecutive days, twenty minutes at a time, about a difficult personal topic. Without much thought, I chose to address my body, or at least "confront" it askance. In these entries I saw just how distasteful and other it was to me.

The hatefulness felt wrong. I was painfully weak. And so I began the work of body awareness demonstrated throughout this book.

What Are You To Me?

August 29

I am my body. My body is I. My body is only a part of my totality, but a major, in-your-face part. Or is it all of who I am? Why speak of parts? That's easy: I don't want to accept it as defining me. I don't want to be decomposition. I hate it! It betrayed me. I'm no fun. Decomposition is my identity now. No, I can't face that. Sometimes I want to kill it. Kill myself?

It was so dependable for years. We climbed anything, jumped down from most anywhere, explored the world, broke sporting records, soared, even. Yes, I felt as if I soared above everything earthly. My body performed just as I intended. A great team!

But we are not two. Or are we? And if not one, how so?

"You are not your body," they scream. Yes, I am, dammit! Why won't you look me in the eye and hold my hand and say it, say that you don't really see me or feel me? Am I like smoke as I go disappearing?

I hear you. "Don't worry. You're not your body anyway." I'd love to separate, but I can't now. I can't, I can't, I can't control you, body, at all! And if I can't control you, I don't want anything to do with you! What are you to me? You betrayed me. But, dammit, you won't just win and leave.

"You're not your body anyway." "You're not your body anyway," they say. Explain! Explain! You make it sound so easy, but I can't separate like you make it sound simple to do and like I want to. Oh, I really want to.

I can't control you, legs, when I stand, having to pause to let tremors shake through you up through my torso. And in bed at night, your muscles fire you into spasms, and I wake so sore, marathon sore. I don't want anything to do with you. But you are I. We are we. I am Rhonda. Am I decay? No!

And what about my eyes, you, eyes, my eyes, eyes that destroyed my photography career? Damn you! And robbed me of ball catching. Damn you! And worst of all, why did they, did you, eyes, have to steal my books? I'd still sit with them, remembering when, lamenting. I'd smell them, finger them, fan my face with pages, but I couldn't explore the world with them, couldn't have the conversations I loved. You robbed me of that community. Damn you! In a vast desert you left me tied to a stake alive, eyes, body. Damn you for betraying me! Damn you! You? Why so separate, so distant? Should I say, damn me? Yes, I hate myself.

August 30

Yesterday's entry was a little bit of a stream-of-consciousness raging against my body. Against me? Huh? I'm not so angry today. I feel more nurturing, like I need to go easy on my body. We have both been betrayed. What? Both? I'm going crazy!

What or who are you to me, I wonder of you, body? I am sad. You are too. Are we one? I can't accept that yet. Let's at least talk.

You work now, eyes, though not perfectly. I can read, and I am so happy and thankful. Sometimes I have to pause in my book and just say, "Thanks." I know that you could leave again at any time. Please stay. MS is hopeful. MS is scary. No guarantees.

Eyes, it must have been so hard for you not to lead me across intersections. Remember that time we almost got hit? It must be frustrating for you when you can't protect me. Remember when we thought that man was following us, but we couldn't really tell? How we hid in the trees and couldn't see around us? And I remember—I'll never forget—how when you returned to me, to yourself, we used to just sit and watch the colors. Remember that? They made us so happy. We cried then. We? Can I use "I"?

You, legs, worked fine when eyes didn't. But then you began to get tired after running four miles, then three miles, then walking four miles, then three, then one, then three blocks, then one, then sometimes you even refused to carry me across the living room. One of you drags now. Do you see people watching us when we step into a room or lurch by them on the street? The cane helps, doesn't it? I'm sorry for you. It must be frustrating as hell when you can't stand, and we have to crawl across the floor. And muscles, you fire when you don't want to.

I'm sad for you. You must hate not being able to play me around a track or through a forest.

August 31

Pennebaker wants this writing practice to lead somewhere: to conclusions or resolutions. But I am still in the throes of your decomposition. Am I decomposition? Is it part of my identity? No! I wish I were an amputee. I could deal with a single problem, find resolution, and then go on living newly from that point. But my resolution has to incorporate the reality of my present, which is rapid corporeal unraveling, and my future, which, most likely, never for sure, is also rapid decomposition. Chronic disease requires the most courageous, flexible living I can imagine. But I don't have to imagine.

The reality of death makes this seemingly extraterrestrial living a possibility and a necessity. Death is present in my everyday. I'm conscious of it always. I take out the trash. Death. I eat chips. Death. I sit silently and watch snow fall. Death. Death. Death. Everybody lives with the same background, but death's presence is easily ignored when a life is running smoothly. I can't ignore it. Is that a luxury? Mystics might think so.

With it so close, though, I think I still have a choice. I can despair or hope. Despair is death-in-life, and hope is choosing life, even when death is so near daily and calls me to follow it mentally, and even physically.

Body, what does this choice for life mean for us? For me? What the fuck is hope?

September 2

This is the last day of Pennebaker's practice. I will have no life-altering conclusion now, but I might have insight that changes how I respond to a given situation or comment or mental state. MS hasn't robbed me of choice. And even if I can't move literally, it hasn't robbed me of action, which I define as assertiveness of my entire person on the world.

My entire person. My entire person? That's body. My entire person is my entire body. I am entirely a body. No experience of day-in, day-out reality for me will be an out-of-body experience. Never!

So I must stop! I must stop taking a dualistic, hack-up-life-into-intelligible-little-pieces approach to my time in time. I need to see my wholeness, feel my wholeness. Body, we are we. Body, we are Rhonda. I am Rhonda, a body. Unthinkable, even Unimaginable.

I'm dizzy.

I'll say it again. Body, we are we. Body, we are Rhonda. I am Rhonda, a body. And when I can get that simple but mind-boggling—body-boggling—truth through my skull of granite and air, maybe I'll soar for real.

Hope. It's what I need to choose over despair if I want to know wholeness. It's a fucking nebulous word, though. What might it mean for me now? Could it mean that in the face of decomposition, of swiftly fading flesh, to hope is to persevere not in expectation of spirit rapture but to persevere as a body—one that smiles, sighs, then disappears?

Body, what are you to me? Body, you, we, I am movement and voice in this life. Body, what are you too? I'll only know by moving, by living.

FREEWRITING

Freewriting (stream-of-consciousness, or spontaneous, writing) is a discipline that works brilliantly against my analytic tendencies for the sake of accessing and incorporating into my written work a texture that results from my body's interaction with the world. Because freewriting highlights more of my immediate self, it's a perfect example of writing. I begin the exercise by using words or images for the initial nudge (like the dream image of a mango or Emily Dickinson's words "Wild nights! Wild nights!"). I give myself time boundaries (five to seven minutes) and let words explode onto a blank page.

The Dream Influence for My Freewrite
I dream about a mango. I'm in a school without walls in the middle of a jungle, and I'm coloring sheets of paper that are full of various blank images. I am giving the images a color according to a diagram that assigns each either red or black. I'm a little frustrated as I follow the diagram closely, but I color by the rules until I get to an image of a mango, which covers almost a whole page. My diagram tells me to make the mango black, but I ignore it. I take out a bright orange marker, begin filling in the mango, and wake in the middle of giving the mango its due color.

The dream was timely. I had to make an important decision the next day: Do I focus precisely on what's required or on my passion?, said the dream. Break rules. Shun what other people require; passion is primary.

For me the mango represents passion. Mangos surrounded me when I lived in Nicaragua, reminders then that I was living outside the rules of what was expected, especially for a woman with a disease. The mango sensually engages the whole body: the color, the flavor, the smell, the texture. A body engaged is a body alive.

Freewrite to the Image of a Mango

The following is a timed freewrite that I began with the image of a mango in my head. After having the dream and doing the freewrite to it, I became convinced that well-being requires the authority of passion, regardless of the rules I might break. My integrity depends on it. A body engaged is a body alive.

Sensual. The mango, orange and so good as I bite in and it drips warm juice down my chin and my arms and falling, falling down my body, but I can't stop laughing and loving and sucking until I am satisfied and I lie back and breathe and feel a little guilty, but the orange is like the blood of another mixing with mine and we are more beautiful and more natural more like light through trees. Orange. Passion? Orange. Hope? Orange. I want orange in my life like a lover, close as breath, so dear. And we touch in ways of eyes and hands and words. We press our orange, our desire near, and we feel the love and feel the soft skin that we were once afraid of but is home now. Orange is home—and the sweetness and smiles and sun that remind us of our fire. Let's make mangos where we sleep and rest and move and love, and let's always laugh at how the juice is not messy, but about living.

DREAMWORK

Dreamwork incorporates the wisdom of my dreams into my waking life. I have most all of my dreams in digesting a book that I have read or a movie that I have seen. I also have dreams as a result of an interaction with another real person. This awareness encourages me to live from my body's fuller knowledge. As I look at my dreams through writing, I consider them in four respects: I write down the dream, I write about how it relates to my present waking life (context), I analyze what I think it means, and I do a timed freewrite to an image from the dream, like the mango dream. Here are three pieces of writing about a different dream.

Skinny-Legged People Dream

I am inside a large house with various women. But as I look through the windows to the dark outside, I see thousands of toothpick legs without knowing to whom they are connected. I know that the skinny-legged people want to invade my house, but I am not fearful or angry. I am just going about my role of keeping them at bay.

However, the skinny-legged people do not try themselves to infiltrate my house. The work is done by men, but is not about violent aggression. They just show up inside, trying to build or construct different things to make way for the skinny-legged people.

My job is to dismantle what they try to build—always feeling very bothered. I remember that one man is trying to erect a high school locker. I just walk off with it.

Then I am leaning over doing something and I feel my hair being batted from behind like a cat hits around a ball. I turn to find a half-man, half-animal crouched and trying to be sexual (that is understood). So for the rest of the dream, I teach the animal how to run its fingers tenderly through my hair, how to treat me like I want to be treated.

Context
- The night before, I had watched the documentary *Dreamworlds,* which portrays how women are objectified in music videos, being reduced to their body parts. At one point of the video, all I could see was a chorus line of skinny legs.
- After I saw the video, going through my mind was a song my mom used to sing to me about a girl named Alice with "legs like toothpicks."
- I saw in the video and in reading *Gyn/Ecology* that men are the henchmen for the oppression of women.
- I continue to wonder about my role regarding body image education for myself, other women, and men.

Analysis
I want to say that the house represents my own body and an invasion by the skinny-legged people would represent an occupation of my body with obsessions like I experienced before. However, I learned from my dream that my battle is against men. The battle is about dismantling what they try to erect in my personal space and about reeducating them about how to treat me.

I think the locker image came up because the video showed that a recurrent theme of male fantasies is sexual encounters with schoolgirls.

I felt no anxiety in the dream. And that's how I feel now with regard to societal threats upon my own body image. I knew what I had to do to protect my house and went about it without too much thought. I think it's important to point out that I wasn't alone in my own house. There were other women around. My dreams lately have tended to be very dualistic regarding men and women.

Reading is more than analyzing and critiquing a book. I think of it as a timeless conversation between bodies, sitting with an author and entreating, "Tell me about the world. Tell me about myself." Many of the feminist authors I have read recently wrote from their entire body. I can tell. I can feel this through my own. I think of their books as gifts to me: They offer their bodies to my body, and, consequently, I have a deeper sense of my own. Sometimes after bringing a book profoundly into my body through writing a literary dialogue, I get teary-eyed, and might even flat-out cry.

Les Guérillères - **Resting with Monique Wittig**

I was once a physical powerhouse, loving to feel in my body the precision and coordination of movement. I felt most myself when playing in trees, shooting a basket, cliff jumping into water, marathon running, skiing, sprinting through the forest, and uniting with nature in the moonlight. Considering my physical past, how ironic that I should read Les Guérillères *on a day that I could hardly move while propped up limp on the couch with megadoses of steroids running through my veins, hoping they would jump-start my body after a multiple sclerosis exacerbation. I read of a band of strong women who play and hunt through the countryside and wage war on the old ways of seeing and doing. Paradoxically, even though my limbs were* immobile as I read, I felt powerful. Not because I was offered an escape from my body, but because as an entire body I felt included.

An early passage describes the living women bringing out a mummy to dry in the sun and returning her inside when rain approaches:

> **The dead woman is clothed in a long tunic of green velvet, covered with white embroidery and gilded ornaments. They have hung little bells on her neck, on her sleeves. They have put medallions in her hair. When they take hold of the box to bring it out the dead woman begins to tinkle everywhere.**

I read the passage. I couldn't move my legs. I cried. I had to use a pillow to hold up the book so I could read more about this circle of women, who were so connected to one another that they attentively put bells on their dead (I like to imagine them all with bells as they take care of one another). The living women in Les Guérillères connect to the dead as if all are part of the same continuum. Death is not a negation or ending. I went tinkling with bells through the rest of the book, better able to imagine my inclusion in such a powerful tribe. My legs wouldn't move. I tinkled on. My arms were numb. I tinkled on. I read and imagined on . . .

Les Guérillères moved me to imagine how I now connect with all women. The tribal women seemed to reach through the pages of the book to touch and hold me ardently, tenderly. They pulled me from my stagnation on the couch into their ring, even though I could hardly stand. I felt that strong women everywhere, ever bonding and banding together for change, were grabbing my hands and including me in their circle of female bodies, whether broken or intact: dancing bodies, moving bodies, fighting bodies, safe bodies, strong bodies. I felt myself joining a powerful community, despite how my legs fell inertly to the floor.

The circle is the recurring symbol that Monique Wittig uses to depict the power of unified women in Les Guérillères. The warriors create the "O" symbol from their own circular vulvas, which reflect the world like a mirror. They use it as a compass to "navigate from sunrise to sunset." "O" is their war cry. Their battle shields are round.

The circle has always appealed to my imagination as a metaphor for community. Monique Wittig's writing invited me to enter and participate in the circle of women. And within this circle, I have realized a depth of community, of joining, that has utterly transformed me.

Without truly knowing our bodies and how they join with other female bodies, I'm convinced that in an important sense we women will remain powerless. For example, because I was once alienated from women (didn't want to be fully associated with the gender because I perceived it as weak), I didn't respect and understand my own intelligence. I would make decisions according to intuition, then apologize for them because they weren't rational. In seeing how I connect with women and in learning to value the nuances of women's intelligence, I have come to have confidence in my own ideas, in my own voice, and in my own movement.

Beware of dispersal. Remain united like the characters in a book. Do not abandon the collectivity. The women are seated on the piles of leaves holding hands watching the clouds that pass outside.

Les Guérillères *allowed me to imagine holding hands in circles of women even when I am dying. Injury and death were such givens for Wittig's warriors (and I could feel their fear and bravery when facing their own mortality) that the maimed, ill, and dead among them were respected, even revered—and never disconnected from the rest. As I lay limp on the couch, my body leapt to imagine the same for myself.*

I want my body to speak to other female bodies about rightful inclusion. I want us each to feel a part of an amazing female community . . . circling . . . and tinkling everywhere.

I am still a physical powerhouse. I just can't move sometimes.

> We are the accumulation of the stories we tell ourselves about who we are . . . Through writing we can revisit our past and review and revise it. What we thought happened, what we believed happened to us, shifts and changes as we discover deeper and more complex truths . . . We use [writing] to shift our perspective.
>
> **louise desalvo, *writing as a way of healing***

Fishing into Manhood

While immersing myself into feminist writing, I felt like I was discovering my female body for the first time. I couldn't help but ask myself an important question: What influenced me to turn away from my gender in the first place? Where did I learn the story that girls were weaker than boys? Wherever I had heard this story, I carried it with me into womanhood, thus remaining alienated from my own body in an important way. This memoir piece explores the male-identified familial world of my youth. As I consider possible body-disregarding influences, I am better able to free a new story to move me.

Fishing made a man of me. Before I could pee standing up, I fished.

Fishing was more a part of my childhood than Straight Flushes, rubber-band-gun wars, The Dukes of Hazzard, and Tastee Freeze. I loved to fish. I lived to fish. And the extended family exchange of inebriated "Big Fish Stories" around the table added the color and texture to our meat-and-potatoes meals.

Fishing in my family was not just here and there, now and then. During the summer, the serious business began every single Friday after dark, with my dog Ginger and me hunting night crawlers through the woods with a flashlight and an old Folgers can half full of dirt. We found worms best by flipping over big rocks and quick-like grabbing them up with a cool handful of dirt, before they could wiggle down their holes.

When Saturday came, my grandparents, Nonnie and Daddy Bob, would fill up their old, green Apache truck with poles, tackle boxes, lawn chairs, coolers, Nonnie's two Chihuahuas, afghan blankets, and a couple of my boy cousins—most all the girls were older or pregnant, even Tina, and she was twelve.

After loading, they would head up our way from their trailer home. Then we'd pile into the truck our own fishing stuff, one cooler, one dog, us three kids, Mom and Dad, more lawn chairs, and one big back seat we'd unbolt from our family Blazer. Seven of us and two big dogs could ride just fine in the truck bed—three on the Blazer seat, pushed back-to-back with the cab. Then we'd head up-valley even farther to Beaver Lake, where I learned the art of angling and the "real man" ways of survival.

"Real men never leave their poles," Daddy Bob would always say as he'd cast his line, take off his shirt, situate a six-pack of Coors in the water, mumble "Goddammit!" now and then so he thought I couldn't hear, and kick back in his lawn chair for the day, munching jalapeño peppers from his pants pocket and drinking one beer after another—which he'd sometimes let me salt for him as I sat on his knee.

Daddy Bob didn't always keep his teeth in his mouth and he coughed something awful (on account of coal dust, Dad said). But he knew all about real men and real men things, being himself a coal miner and a fisherman—just like my dad and his dad.

Great Grandpa, he never moved well enough to fish by the time I knew him, but everybody always said he was the best, that he could "hook 'er up real good!" I do remember how he'd come visiting with quarters in his pockets so he could lean on his walker, toss them in the air, and laugh as all us kids dove and fought for them. They called him "Dinosaur Jack" because he was so drunk one night on the way home from a bar that he swore he saw dinosaurs on the high school football field—"not them girly long-neck-ed ones," so the story went. Great Grandpa scared me sometimes, but not on account of drinking too much—real men always did.

"We Henderson men, we like our beer!" Daddy Bob would say. And he taught me about how real men have to fight in bars sometimes if they don't wanna be sissies. Real men hide Coors around the yard for when they mow the lawn. Real men listen to Hank Williams. And real men never wear shoes or shirts when fishing.

"Daddy Bob," I said one day, as I set up in my usual fishing spot between him and Dad, "Do real men wear fingernail polish on their toes like you?"

Since real men fished without shoes, I couldn't miss his pink polished toes as he wiggled them in the sun.

"Real men like me do, sweetheart," he said.

"Why?" I asked.

"Honey, I'm just darin' my buddies at work to call me a woman—so I can beat the . . . beat 'em up 'long side the head. You know, beat 'em so they don't know what's comin'!"

My cousin Greg told me that Daddy Bob was lying, that he really painted his toenails for easy body identification if the mine caved in. I never wore polish.

I had Greg to one side of my fishing spot when I couldn't be next to Daddy Bob. He always wore really high baseball hats with pictures of farm machines. Swore he'd work one when he got older. He was usually really stupid, but that was no matter to me since I could just keep my mind to fishing if I wanted to ignore him.

But sometimes we messed around, like when we made fun of our cousins from over the mountain, the ones that fished with bobbers. Bobbers?! We'd offer them our night crawlers, but they wanted to float their little red ping-pong ball thingies, which made us laugh together.

Real fishermen didn't use bobbers.

And Greg and I for the longest time wondered why the dragonflies buzzed around piggy-back like that, until he figured it out one day.

"Rhonda, thems must be screwin'."

I always caught more fish than Greg, which made him spit and watch his pole more. As the day went on, he'd usually start calling me girl names and make fun of how I talked.

"Why do you gotta always put ends on all yer words all the time?" he'd say to me. "You haveta' always talk, 'fish-ING fish-ING.' Ain't nobody here 'fish-ING.' We're all 'fishin'.' 'Fishin'.' Talk like normal folks. Yer soundin' like a girly girl."

And he'd go on sometimes about how I would never have hair on my chest like real men and how I could never ever go exploring with him to the Bermuda Triangle, since I was a girl and might be too scared and scream all the time at stupid things. But he said that since I wasn't "growed up" yet into a "wo-man," he would still hang out with me while we fished.

But because I wasn't big yet, I didn't pay Greg any mind when he teased me about being "female." He couldn't really call me a girl—couldn't prove it! I wasn't anything like them, and never would be! I never ran like one or threw a ball like one or played with dolls like one or wore dresses like one. Never!

"Treat me like a boy!" I'd always demand of everyone. Couldn't Greg and all the rest see that I did lots of things even better than boys—especially fishing!

Mom was God to me—except she was a girl—and she made the best PB&J ever! She'd just about kill herself trying to call me away from my lawn chair to eat something, but everybody knew that real men never left their poles. I was always the best fisherman of all the kids. I had to be, since the day I stopped fishing, was the day I became a girl, was the day I packed lunches for the fisherMEN, was the day that life must be over.

"No, Mom," I'd whine. "I'm scared I'll miss something if I look away."

I always made sure that I fished next to Dad. I liked the way he smelled when we were at the lake—like dirt and salmon eggs. And he knew I was a real fisherman, being his "official partner," he said. He would help Jason and Jeremy too, but they were never serious like me.

He'd cut, untangle, and load things when I asked him to—but I never needed much help. I would cast my pole all myself too. I never salted his beer, but he'd save me some sips at the end of each of his—and I'd hold the can for a while after as I watched my line.

Whenever I caught a fish, I liked to kill it without Dad's help. He taught me to whack, whack, whack its head across a rock until its tailfin stopped wiggling back and forth. Sometimes Dad himself didn't even whack his own before he stuck his thumb into the fish's mouth, pointer finger around the back of its neck, and then ripped back its head. I couldn't do this. I had to kill it before I ripped its head off.

I wanted to be just like Dad. But even though I kept my hair short and played with Tonka Trucks, he never noticed how much I was really like a boy.

"Young lady, put your shirt back on right now!" he said all of a sudden one day.

For so long, I fished topless like the boys, before Dad started calling me "young lady" and expected me to "act like one"—which I thought must be a bad thing.

"But, Daaaaad!"

"No buts!" he'd say. "You're too old for that! Runnin' around like a wild girl!"

After putting the shirt back on, I would spit and burp more than before as I caught the most and the biggest fish. When I started wearing shirts, he paid me less attention. So if I couldn't completely control the whims of my body and get his eye by looking like a boy, I'd certainly impress him with what I could accomplish like a boy. Better than a boy!

After a day on the lake, all of us burned up bright red like Nonnie's lipstick, we dragged to my house for poker, more beer, an "out-of-doors" fish fry, and lotsa' fishing stories. Daddy Bob would almost always tell us how he had to jump in the lake after his pole that same day.

"Half up to my neck!" he'd say. "The slimy s.o.b. trout—monster, that one—almost dragged my s.o.b. pole out to where I wouldn't never see it no more!" Largest he'd seen in years!

When Uncle Donny was there, someone always told his fishing story, of how when he was younger, he won the drugstore Big Fish Contest by stealing his winner one night from the town fish hatchery. Police never did catch him.

After the women went inside to do their things and we fishermen were just resting by the fire, sometimes something about the night and about being real men together made us feel like singing our family song, "Put Another Log on the Fire" (Shel Silverstein).

COMMUNAL EXPRESSION

When I hear the words of other women, their voices and subjects free my own unique and communal voice to tell my similar stories, to uproot buried silences. At times I feel like a participant in a lovely communal release, feel like my hand is being held gently by a friend assuring me, "It's okay. It's okay," as I join my body with hers and share my experience: reclaiming, deploring, celebrating.

Steamy

In writing the following piece after seeing a production of *The Vagina Monologues*, I was taking my place in *The Vagina Monologues* community. The verbal expression of other women freed my own telling of this story. After hearing my story, other women have responded with tales of their own experience of pleasure. So far, my story has reached eight countries and much of the U.S.! I'm amazed at the unity realized by just a little bit of open expression, just a little reclamation of pleasure.

My vagina has stories, too, I insisted to myself after seeing a Vagina Monologues *performance. I thought, how hard could it be to tell my own? After all, I went to that erotic writing workshop and yelled out socially taboo words with only mildly inhibited gusto. Why not celebrate my socially taboo vagina also?*

Well, I've put off the writing for about three weeks now. Almost daily, I wake with fresh boldness, announcing to Mike something like, "Today, I'm going to write a vagina monologue."

At first he was turned on, but after time he just grinned and nodded and teased, "Put your vagina where your mouth is."

I'd just smart-ass back, "I'd rather put it where yours is." (How's that for warm-up?)

Okay, here goes. It's erotica, yes, but not the skin-on-skin type. It's steamier!

My official sex ed. began young—at four. Cindy showed me how babies are made. She grabbed her Baby Tenderlove and Baby Wet 'Ems, took off all their clothes, and pressed them up close so their chests and faces were mashed together.

"Pretend this is one boy and one girl," she said. She told me more, too, and I couldn't believe that our parents were so icky! I started spreading the horrible news: "Did you know that moms and dads make babies by getting naked and peeing all over each other?"

Then, after I caught Mom and Dad in all that mess like Cindy described, Mom got out her "doctor" book. She pointed to a funny drawing with lots of curlicued squiggles all over the privates and said something like, "Honey, this is cop-you-lay-shun. Boys and girls don't do this till they're at least 21—usually older. Never when they're little. It's for making babies."

A couple years later when I was six, some high school boys took me behind a dumpster and touched and kissed me in the place the drawing showed. I began to hate and to ignore down there, until sixth grade.

Sixth grade was the dawning of vagina awareness, since it began giving me lots of trouble. I just couldn't ignore it in middle school like I had. For one thing, the wild hair took some getting used to. I remembered the picture squiggles. But the really strange thing about my vagina was how it throbbed at slumber parties whenever I watched movies of boys and girls "doing it." It went crazy, but I loved how it felt—like fire!

Enter . . . the shower massager.

Until eighth grade, a shower was basically about doing time—cleaning up—then getting out. But the day I discovered I could remove the showerhead, I became a woman.

The corporeal conversion happened when I got myself all lathered up, and then casually perused my soapy body with the gyrating stream. Neck ... armpits ... torso ... feet ... legs ... crotch ... hmm ... crotch ... hmm?! Crotch ... more and more ... soap gone, but don't ... want ... to ... stop ... mmm ... pulsing water, warm and beating, warm and beating ... oh ... longer, longer ... longer, longer ... ahh ... mmm ... throbbing, throbbing ... and ... cir-cle-ing and cir-cle-ing ... and ohmygosh, ohmygosh ... beat of fire, beat of fire ... more and more and more and more and oh and oh ... oooo ... ooooo ... and ... and ... and ... huh ... huh, huh, huh, huh ... Ahhhhhhhhhh ....

Imagine my all-over shock, having never heard of that kind of bodily ... thing. I couldn't even give words to the experience (then). It was pure experience for me the first time, then pure the second time, then pure again and again and ...

"Why do you spend so much time in the shower, honey?" asked Mom.

"It's warm," I'd answer.

Then, when Mom took Jason, Jeremy, and me to the church's "Sex Night," I learned the real story about my vagina. Pastor Dan stood up front while we slouched in the pews, and he went on and on about ..."FORNICATION!"

"Rhonda, what's 'fornication'?" Jeremy whispered.

"Doing it."

I learned that fornication was a really bad thing to do before marriage. I learned it was bad to even fornicate "in our hearts," to even think about doing it in the first place. Was I fornicating "in my heart" in my shower? There in the pews, I hunched even more as I learned that I was a sinner. I had left the house clean and pure, but I returned home that night a horribly evil fornicator! God most definitely hated me for how I showered!

Soon after I learned that I was a sinner, Mom began to leave Christian dating books on my dresser. They told me the same story that Pastor Dan had about my dirtiness. I felt so terrible ... but it felt so good ... so I felt terrible ... then it felt good ... and so on and so on, ad infinitum—*until that hellish day when Dad stepped from the bathroom with the shower massager—my shower massager—strung around his neck like some sort of trophy anaconda.*

"Hi Dad!" I was so casual. "Whatcha' doin' with the shower massager?"

"It broke. Gotta get a new one."

"Will it . . . uh . . . be . . . removable?" So casual.

"Nope," he said. "No, I'll just get the stay-put kind. Don't need to be gettin' fancy about how the water comes out."

Then he walked out the door with my first love flung limply across his shoulder.

"Honey, you never used to take baths," Mom said.

"They're warm," I answered, leaving out the part about how I would lie on my back and throw my legs up over the spigot end of the free-standing tub for just one more go . . . just one . . . only one more . . . one . . . more . . . just . . . this . . . one . . . last . . . ahhhhhhhhhhhh.

My high school sex life was . . . clean. Kids knew me as "the virgin," but I couldn't figure out why they taunted me, when they were the ones worrying about venereal diseases, pregnancy, and the all-around messiness of relationships. But we were all really the same anyway: all fornicators. I was just a private one. I had sexual problems too. If I let the water get too hot . . . ouch!

Scalding aside, my biggest issue was the shame—the shame born of high school boys taking me behind a dumpster when I was six; the shame of being taught about the sin of fornicating in my heart; the shame from reading dating books that spoke to me of a purity that negated my bathing habits; the shame of feeling a burning down there but being unable to make it stop. I tried and tried to end the trysts, even using various autodisciplinary techniques. I was very serious about taming my vagina.

Okay, I'd say to myself, if I don't masturbate today, I can have ice cream. But that didn't work, since I'd masturbate and then have ice cream. When food prizes failed to motivate me, I tried keeping a masturbation calendar, just to mark off how many days I could go without doing it. That road also led to ice cream and to continued self-loathing. For years, I claimed that each romp in the tub was definitely my last.

Ridiculous mind games like this went on and on for a few years. My well-being, I thought, depended on taming my irritatingly impetuous vagina, my horrible, wonderful . . . horrible.

..wonderful...here...I...go...again...ahhhhhhhhhhhhhh........

But I couldn't ever really enjoy the sensations of my body, because when I felt "good," I also felt "bad."

How sad, really sad that it took me so long to learn the rule of pleasure. Simple rule. Wonderfully simple. Simply, how do I love and respect myself silly? What makes my whole body feel really good? That's it. Simple. So all I really have to do is to sink my awareness into pure sensation and into pure emotion, mature enough to abandon myself freely and safely to a whole body experience, while being on-guard not to slip so easily into the abstract and dizzying theories I mentioned earlier, the god-awful proclamations that gave me permission to writhe and moan—and to enjoy it. Permission to feel my body! Permission? Permission? It seems to me that the only "slippery slope" of pleasure leads not to guilt but to happiness.

Mike and I walked through Home Depot recently, planning to ready our new house with some basic amenities. In the shower section, I picked up a simple hand-held sprayer to put into our bathtub without a shower spigot. Mike very assertively grabbed it out of my hand and replaced it with a multi-speed, "super turbo" massager. We looked at one another and smiled.

II

BODY TO BODY
Connecting with Women

Women alone stir
my imagination.

**virginia woolf, letter to ethel
smythe, august 19, 1930**

Put back your body where your life belongs.
sara suleri, *meatless days*

Until my early thirties, I wasn't very interested in women.

I had good, valued friends, but if I wanted to have what I thought was an intellectual conversation, I went to men. I'll use the example of writers to explain: I tried and tried, but fiction written by women didn't interest me much. Over the years, I only read a smattering of their works, and I was so bored by them that in order to give some examples here, I would now have to go dig for names and titles in my bookshelf—assuming I didn't take them to a used bookstore. I remember Toni Morrison, though. I read all of her books, but I recall feeling left out by them, like they weren't talking to me about me.

I could relate better to male authors. I'll mention a few. Albert Camus blew my mind. *The Plague* was my favorite book for many years, as it spoke to me of illness and well-being. Dostoyevsky's *Brothers Karamazov* dazzled me before *The Plague*. I enjoyed its thoughtful challenging of theological givens, and the one-dimensional female characters and their "fainting spells" were easy for me to overlook. Finally, Cormac McCarthy's *Blood Meridian* delighted my ear and intellect. I was the only woman I knew who liked the book. Even though I was part of a women's book club in my late twenties—I liked the food and the general conversation—the female-written book choices bored me. I can't even remember any to list here.

This sets up the dismal background for my awakening. Within a short amount of time, I read three books of women's memoir, since I was planning to do my own memoir writing. The first was Jo Ann Beard's *The Boys of My Youth*. I liked it. There was something oddly accessible to me about it, and that surprised me. Being a woman is important to her. Hmm . . .

After Beard, I continued with two more books recommended to me. Eva Hoffman's *Lost in Translation* caused me great excitement as I read. I related so much to her life, despite the fact that she was a Polish immigrant to Canada: her themes of alienation and of self-discovery through language, as well as her general experience of being female. Our deep connection spanned cultures.

Finally, the book that sent me running to read more about my own body, specifically in feminism, was Sara Suleri's *Meatless Days*. She writes about growing up in Pakistan. I'm from a mountain town in Colorado, but she was talking about my experience while sharing hers: about life in a male-centered atmosphere and about the difference between male and female perspectives and approaches to the world. I felt excited and newly enlivened as I read, and I didn't want to stop!

Sara Suleri says in *Meatless Days,* "Put back your body where your life belongs." The sentence was cryptic to me because she seemed to be suggesting that my body might not be a genuine part of my life at all. Though I could look in the mirror and prove otherwise, her phrase entranced me, and I needed to figure out what she could mean.

Because the writing of these women had begun to cause me to feel new stirrings in my body, I knew what first step to take: a comprehensive delving into feminist literature. Putting back my body into my life, I thought, required contextualizing it. Even though I had historically not identified with women in many ways, I wanted to learn what it meant to be female. More importantly, as I got deeper into the writing, I learned how it *felt* to embrace my identity as female. It felt like passion had taken my whole body ardently into its arms and wasn't ever going to let me go again.

To say that reading women's literature and feminist theory was a time of awakening is to say that I felt how my body joined with a community of other bodies, past and present, and that joining was life-shattering. I was contextualized, and as a result I began to live differently. I planned a project of photographing women; I facilitated writing workshops that made a space for women only; and I continued to read more and more written by women, since their words seemed to be reflecting me more honestly than any mirror ever had.

I open this section with a confession piece I wrote before beginning to read feminism. If it doesn't suggest that I had been living a radically disempowered life before studying feminism, it's because I hadn't. But after the exploration, I could knowledgeably claim the title of "feminist" and could also explain much of my former existence in feminist terms. With a fuller sense of my identity, I began moving into new experiences with awareness of my female body. Wow!

This "Body to Body" section is an eclectic tribute to women and to being female. Erinn and Lise are friends. I include here my reflective responses to quotes from female writers, a personal essay on body awareness, and a memoir piece about feeling responsibility toward a Nicaraguan woman.

The discipline of grounding myself as female, of learning to feel my female body and how it joins with others, has been the most body- and life-changing awareness practice of all. This section is a tribute to awareness of my femaleness.

In connecting and identifying with women, I started to feel my body more acutely. I was learning what it meant to put back my body where my life belongs.

FEMINIST THEORY
Grounded!

> Feminist theory is grounded in experience; I have always
> written feminist political and philosophical analysis from the
> bottom up, starting with my own encounters and adventures,
> frustrations, pain, anger, etc.
>
> **marilyn frye**

Joining

I'm sitting in some hellish window light. I smell the coffee and hear the espresso machine. The door squeaks as people move in and out. I look up every time, because I'm not too interested in what I'm doing.

I have chai . . . and my laptop . . . and I'm slouching back in my chair . . . limply. My energy is spent, and I don't much feel like moving in any direction: into reading, into writing, into anything. When I'm not watching the door swing open or twisting my mug with my right hand, I keep staring at the brick wall and thinking that the black and white photographs hanging there are . . . blah!

I have a book. It's in my lap mostly, but I pick it up here and there to look at the cover. I open it too, but have only a little bit of attention for it in quick flashes, before I have to stop and consider those ugly photographs; or the maddening sun through the glass, with its saccharine perkiness seeming so out of place juxtaposed with my book and my body. I slouch.

I read the cover again: *The Birth of Pleasure*. Carol Gilligan is obviously sharp, and she says some good things about . . . well . . . pleasure . . . and about . . . well . . . body fragmentation . . . and all that. But it's missing something for me. Damn sun! Horrible photographs! *I'm* missing something. I notice a crack in my mug, from lip to base.

I pick up the book and put it down again. Maybe because I'm limp, or maybe because I'm bored, I remember a time when I wasn't either. I remember my passion from a few months earlier, passion that impelled me to write, "I feel like making love to the world, and I feel like the world is making love to me." The memory makes me laugh a little, considering the light through the window and my body so limply in it. But wasn't my passion about light and body in the first place? Didn't the words of feminist authors reveal my body to me, cause me to feel it newly? New awareness of my body was my "birth of pleasure." What does Carol Gilligan have to offer me now?

Here with the obnoxious sun across my body and a lifeless-to-me book in my lap, I remember the promise that took me through the summer. I swore to keep passion as the measure of all I do. It was really quite simple, and not so hard to practice, as passion was already impelling me to act with new vision and responsibility toward other women. Why am I here like this now? Did I forget something?

I reach into my wheelchair backpack, because I think I must still be carrying a book by Marilyn Frye. I find it, open it, and begin reading "To Be and Be Seen: The Politics of Reality." I hope the essay will remind me of what I forgot.

After a page—only one page—I sit up in my chair, and the light through the windows seems softer.

I read, "The event of becoming a lesbian is a reorientation of attention in a kind of ontological conversion." To be called a lesbian, she says, is more a matter of perceptual rather than sexual orientation.

A woman walks through the door, and I notice her thick make-up and black leather jacket. I imagine her without the cover-up. That's what my ontological conversion provokes, I think. I want to see women exposed. I want to be exposed too. I better understand my motives for my photography project, why I turned toward women with such attention: I'm a lesbian (female-identified).

"Attention is a kind of passion," says Frye.

I put the book down because the words overwhelm me: so truthful, they hurt! I feel like my body is on fire. In this public place with this book, I love to feel it leap with such power. I again consider my identity as a lesbian.

Erasure, says Frye, is about diverting "the eye, the attention, and the mind."

I lower the book again. I look down at my body. I used to ignore so much of it, and I hated what I did see and feel: I remember the eating disorder and my aversion to mirrors. How is that possible, I think now, with Marilyn Frye speaking to me? I see myself because I know I am seen.

As I feel my body burning, I also see it starkly, right here in this chair. I don't turn away. The sun falls through the window as if its purpose is to reveal me. Though I'm sitting, my legs are spread sturdily across the tiled floor. I put my hands on them, one on each leg, elbows shooting out to the sides. I see and feel how I occupy this space.

To love women, says Frye, is to see women with one's eyes, attention, and attachment. It is to see that women have senses of their own, have perceptual authority, and have a unique point of view. Loving women is not seeing women as objects for use, ones known only in relation to the norm, but as subjects with souls.

Two college girls walk in. They look alike: same hair hanging blonde and straight down their backs, same Jansport backpack on the same left shoulder, same way they tilt their heads to the right and swing their arms in unison. As I sit in this revelation of window light, leaning on my arms over my strong legs, I feel sad for them. Their movement is not strong or unique. They walk in stride, but they seem more separate than joined.

Here with my book that straightens my back, strengthens my legs, focuses my sight, transforms the light, and tells me a story about myself so honestly that I can read only a little bit at a time, I feel responsible to the women. I imagine chasing them down and telling them the same story that Marilyn Frye just retold me, a story about their bodies that is truer than their identical shoes and their matching cell phones.

I watch the girls walk away. Although I don't chase them, maybe I will sit with others like them some day. I continue to feel so aflame, pick up the Carol Gilligan book again, and find things I never would have seen earlier when my body was so limp and disengaged from the light:

> To free love and pleasure . . . means to undo dissociation by risking association—knowing what one knows, feeling one's feelings, being naked in the presence of another.
>
> **carol gilligan, *the birth of pleasure***

CONFESSIONS OF A WANNABE FEMINIST

You have to be strong to be vulnerable.

lise weil, quoting the painter joan mitchell, in *trivia 15*

I Am Not a Feminist.

How can I be? I don't really know what the word means. A feminist friend tells me that I am, but that news only makes me feel ashamed and curious. I don't know my history as a woman. I haven't even read or liked much of the literature of women. I feel as if I have spent most of my life trying to be "as good as the boys." I am not worthy of the title, but I want to be. I feel as if the title calls to me to embrace it, to explain it, and to use it as a word that describes my existence to myself and to others.

I Am Attracted to Strong Women.

Sharp women. I am attracted in most every way. I want to talk forever with them about our bodies. I desire intimacy. I know a strong woman when I see one. Strength is about the directions in which a woman turns her face to see the world and about how she moves her body to engage it.

I Am Weak When . . .

I let *them* get in my head and influence my thoughts and movement. I can plug my ears, but my mind is hard to stop as it races down well-grooved tracks that tell me to place parts of myself outside and beyond. Who are they? Ghosts with power over things they can't really grasp? Ghosts that become flesh when named? In the naming, they lose the strength to bend even a daisy.

I Am Strong When . . .

I see and I name and I move without ropes attached to dead things.

Bruising, Pained, and Screaming, Voiceless . . .

I once went for a bumper ride through hell?

I Used to Think My Life Began . . .

Where my flesh ended. Now I'm learning that it began where my female body began. This truth really blew my mind at first and disorients me still. Might I one day find my body wandering some back alley of my presently shadowed history?

I Am Afraid . . .

Of where my questions might lead, but fear is a part of any question that leads to fuller life. I am afraid of familial indifference to the transformed me, but I should be more afraid of my own indifference to myself.

I Am Not Afraid . . .

Of much when I'm not afraid of everything. I lust to put myself in scary situations and to ask the scary questions. I know the potential of insecurity. Growth and strength are born from experience and risk.

Menstruation...

Was shameful early on. When I bled for the first time, I locked the bathroom door, pulled out those funny Mom things from under the sink, read the instructions that diagramed how to raise one leg on the toilet, got scared of insertion, and so wore pads till college. I sometimes wonder if I have left the world of diagrams. I don't wonder if I have left a bathroom steeped with aloneness and shame.

I Didn't Want to Eat...

In college, but I hated myself long before that. For four years I denied myself food of every sort. I am only now learning to feed myself.

Death...

I thought once, must be the only alternative to not being like the girls in beer commercials.

I Was Ashamed When...

They took the guys away to talk to them about masturbation. I don't remember what we discussed.

I Was So Free When...

I swam nude in Bali. I threw off my clothes as if they had been choking me for a lifetime. Eyes everywhere, but I had something to do.

I Never Paid Much Attention...

To my sexuality. I was a master suppressor. They called me a lesbian in high school, so I was asexual. They called me a sinner in college, so I was asexual.

One "Relationship" . . .

Is all I have had . . . ever.

I Didn't Believe Them When They Told Me . . .

I couldn't, so I did. However, not in the name of *my own* success or of a woman's success, but in the name of success *like* men's. "A girl can't run and climb trees and build cities with Tonka Trucks like a boy," they said. Then I did. "A girl can't handle a ball like a boy," they said. Then I did. "A woman can't think with the precision of a man," they said. So now I am thinking with the creativity of a woman: precision and more!

I'm Married and I Changed My Name.

"Double Whammy," some say. I love Mike. I love his last name too, which is mine. I hated my former name—or was it the name only? I never considered whom I might lose, and still can't say that it was anybody—any body. Rhonda Henderson. Rhonda Henderson. I don't even know who she was before she became the person I am only beginning to recognize now.

I Feel Good . . .

About my past integrity of knowledge, voice, and action. And still now, I don't doubt their camaraderie in my life. That excites me.

I Want to Understand . . .

The difference between "empowerment" and "independence." I am dependent. I am strong.

I Have Never . . .

Faked an orgasm. I hate to fake anything.

Now That I Can't Control It . . .
I love my body more than ever.

Disease Weakened Me . . .
To the roots of my strength.

FEMINISTS

The poet Muriel Rukeyser once asked, "What would happen if one woman told the truth about her life?" Her answer: "The world would split open." And so it has. A revolution is under way, and there is no end in sight.

ruth rosen, *the world split open*

I was born in early 1969, a time when women all across the United States were laying powerful minds and hands on the nation and shaping it into my new home, a home where I grew up expecting certain freedoms without barriers. I assumed equality with boys and men in education, work, athletic opportunities, and social inclusion. Always. And only now, after reading *The World Split Open,* do I know my ideological mothers for the first time. I am humbled, realizing that my freedom did not begin with myself. I am not at all shaken because things in my life have been withheld from me, but floored by the knowledge that these liberties were won by the unflagging work of women. In fact, my former feelings of radical independence are really a betrayal, since how and where I move has always been contingent on an impressive feminist timeline that radically split the world open enough for me to confidently jump in.

I am so thankful to them.

Dream

I am among a small group of familiar women who are exchanging gifts. I'm surprised to open one that contains several long, blue, and cylindrical candles. All but a couple are lit. I move around the lively room, asking each person by name if she had given me the gift. Each says, no, until I ask Lise. "Yes," she says, and rushes to relight the candles that have died.

Meditation

I had a conversion time reading feminism.

I have heard that reading feminism for the first time can result in an ontological upheaval. God yes! I have never felt as passionate as when I read female writers writing about my body. They locate it, so I locate it and feel it, and it feels good—like really living. I'm burning now just thinking about what I know.

How fitting that Lise's dream gift to me is flames. I'll always credit her for giving me the initial gift of feminism, the gift of my body. I probably wouldn't have read it apart from her passion for it. She loves women. I needed to have her confidence and perspective behind and before me. After so many years of blinders, I needed sight training in order to face the world on my own, as a woman.

Thank you, Lise.

AUDRE LORDE DREAM

I love what Lorde elicits in you! She would have loved it too.

lise weil, letter

Dream

At some unknown location with vast interiors and exteriors, I am hugging and saying goodbye to all sorts of women from my past. We meet, we hug, and I go on to others. Then a black woman approaches me, and without speaking, we both know we have something deep between us. We hug with intensity, and then I hold her hand and start stroking her head tenderly. Suddenly, she starts crying and leaves. I look after her, but she has disappeared. I hurt so deeply from her departure that I begin wailing mournfully and wake myself crying.

Meditation

Yes, the black woman could represent me—an alter ego of sorts, the part that is dying and leaving suddenly. However, I really want to think she represents Audre Lorde. I feel very tenderly toward her after my experience of journal writing to some of her quotes from *The Cancer Journals.* For several days, I recently sat with and conversed with her intimately through writing. I feel such companionship in bravely living fully while facing mortality. I have never had these vital conversations with anybody. The dream, I think, expresses the connection I feel.

Why did I cry when we parted? Loss? Maybe I cried because I need models that meet me corporeally, who, in a way, see me and let me see them. Maybe I feel so alone with my will to live fully, despite disease. Maybe I cried because I never knew Audre Lorde when she was alive. Maybe I am just mourning her death for the first time. Maybe . . .

Timed Freewrite with the Whole Audre Lorde Dream in Mind

I'm sorry I never knew you before. We can't hold hands now, but I hold you where I live, and you water me as I grow, and I hope I am beautiful for what you gave me and give me, and I will never forget you now that I know how you moved. Mothers. Sisters. Guides. Sun. Water. I grow. We grow in me in all women we grow and the world laughs and cries and smiles on the beauty and passion. Hello and goodbye and aren't we beautiful, aren't we strong and don't we make the trees green and the world rest a little more? We run through sun to the beautiful places that can bear our brilliant countenances. Let passion run me around the earth into your arms!

When I read *The Cancer Journals,* I rested. I was not alone in my fear or passion, in my despair or lust for life. I rested. I breathed. My following meditations are spontaneous outpourings in response to Audre Lorde's words.

Where are the models for what I'm supposed to be in this situation?

Where Are the Models?

I sometimes feel like I am so alone. Other people have MS, but nobody with MS is like me. Proud, yes, but it's true. I haven't met a photographer who was a former runner who loved to bake bread—a former me as a former mover. But when have I ever met somebody like me at all? When have I ever had a model of that caliber? Hasn't my whole life been improvisation? What's changed, except that I can't even keep up the illusion of following behind?

As I read Lorde's words, I wasn't alone. Her love for and commitment to women seems to seep through every sentence she writes. She's a model for that reason, but that's not it. She entered my life at this time when I'm not only desperate for female models, but I need to have somebody hold my hand and say, "See, Rhonda, this is how we live wholly and passionately, despite the disintegration of our bodies."

She was fearful of cancer, and she admitted it. At the same time, she was powerfully engaged in living. I feel so much stronger and happier for admitting my fear, while having vision for how my diseased body can still move powerfully.

I wish I could tell her how much of a support she has been.

> *How do you spend your time, she said. Reading, mostly, I said. I couldn't tell her that mostly I sat staring at blank walls, or getting stoned into my heart, and then, one day when I found I could finally masturbate again, making love to myself for hours at a time. The flame was dim and flickering, but it was a welcome relief to the long coldness.*

Making Love to Myself

I cried when I first read these words. They're my favorite in this book, some of my favorite ever. I know she's talking specifically about masturbation, but the quote speaks to me of her strong desire to live, while still being pulled by her health into despair. I feel the same conflicting desires: sometimes to die, but also to live with intensity.

I want to learn to make love to myself, even while my body comes apart, which is not to say that I'll continue to masturbate only. Having addressed Lorde's literal meaning, I think that making love to my entire self is about claiming the right to live fully. After so much time of courting blank walls—places of no color, no vision, all limit—making love to myself is about creation, pleasure, passion, possibility, movement. Writing the pieces in this book, I was making love to myself. Learning to feel and understand myself as a body, I am making love to myself. Seeing women as if for the first time, I am making love to myself. Facing my own mortality honestly, I am making love to myself.

More than literal death, I fear a life in which I stop making love to myself—in every way.

A mastectomy is not a guilty act that must be hidden in order to regain acceptance or protect the sensibilities of others. Pretense has never brought about lasting change or progress.

Incontinence

Pretense is powerlessness. After her mastectomy, Lorde walked around one-breasted in order that other women with a mastectomy would recognize her and approach her openly. She also wanted all of society to be more aware of the experience of so many women. How essential! She didn't want to hide her body's reality just to protect the sensibilities of others, thus perpetuating a disconnection from mortality.

When Lorde speaks of overcoming societal silences as essential for personal and communal well-being, I automatically think incontinence. I have begun to speak more openly about incontinence. Bladder problems are early symptoms of most every person with MS. However, whenever I participate in MS seminars or events, the speaker usually addresses incontinence with whispers or more or less obvious discomfort.

Because I feel hurt and angry by this shame-reinforcing silence, I have begun talking about incontinence matter-of-factly with other MSers—which is liberating. Now I mention to people who know me that incontinence is part of my experience. I want my friends to start seeing that someone they know and like can live with a terribly socially taboo condition.

The challenge now for me is to free the silence enough to make incontinence socially acceptable. In order to be more visible, I purposefully walk through the store with my package of 60 incontinence pads tucked under an arm. People probably guess they're for a grandparent. They would never think that a nice, young woman would need *those*. We're everywhere, though! So why do we sometimes feel dirty or guilty? As Lorde says, the isolation of hiding is disempowering. At least *I'm* beginning the process of "coming out."

I'm so tired of all this. I want to be the person I used to be, the real me. I feel sometimes that it's all a dream and surely I'm about to wake up now.

Tired of This!

Nostalgia is inevitable when I feel like I am on my second life, but still hang onto parts of the first like icons. The charm of reincarnation is forgetfulness. I can't forget, but often I want to. I am guilty of feeling sorry for myself, of trying to imagine my life now if it weren't for . . . Like Lorde, I'm so tired of this present situation sometimes, lots of the time. I want to run, ski, drive, walk up the stairs, dream . . . dream . . .

But I am more the real me now than I ever was. And I would never want to go back to my padded walls, knowing how alive I am when I feel the abrasions and hit my head on things. The ever-present reality of death keeps me awake and moving. I'm happy now when I can muster enough bravery and vision to look upon my past with both tenderness and "good riddance!" My present is not a negation of my past. It joins with it to form my life—a full one.

I do not forget cancer for very long, ever. That keeps me armed and on my toes, but also with a slight background noise of fear.

If I can remember to make the jump from impotence to action, then working uses the fear as it drains it off, and I find myself furiously empowered.

Background of Fear

MS is not such a big, fearful deal when I am passionate. Passion seems to fell all boundaries, especially the energy-binding ones we erect between life and death. But I don't work myself into some sort of crazy-woman ecstasy, just so I can forget that my feet are numb and my left leg has gone inert. The passion that propels me to action, I think, comes from how my body moves and doesn't move. It comes from MS and the background of fear.

Hmm . . . lately for me, fear engenders passion, and then passion drains it off.

I really don't think that I could be so furiously empowered without the way I am dying.

My visions of a future I can create have been honed by the lessons of my limitations.

Realistic Limit

But my challenge as I create a future for myself is to separate real limit from fear-imposed limit. Fear is the great erector of limit. For example, after my photography business folded due to MS, I didn't want to return to school and work toward another vocation, because I feared that my desires would be blocked again. This limit I erected was fear imposed.

Realistically, I can't train for the Ironwoman. Fear-istically, I can't be an ironwoman. Realistically, I can't do it alone. Fear-istically, I can't do it at all. Realistically, I can't stand sometimes. Fear-istically, I can't stand against what I think is harmful to bodies. Realistically, I sometimes have trouble moving my limbs. Realistically, I can't stop my intellect and my imagination and my growth and my relationships and my words and my words and my words . . .

If I do what I need to do because I want to do it, it will matter less when death comes, because it will have been an ally that spurred me on.

When Death Comes

I think about death daily, sometimes despairingly, but mostly now to remind me that I am still alive and that while I can still walk to the mailbox, I want to; while I can still connect with women and photograph their bodies, I am honored to; while I can still incite imagination in others, I love to; while I can still hold hands, face lightward and bleed passion, I am living.

> *. . . and either I would love my body one-breasted now, or remain forever alien to myself.*

Loving a Diseased Body

Alienation from my body is death in life.

The following is a literary dialogue with Susan Griffin's words from her feminist classic, *Woman and Nature: The Roaring Inside Her.* The essay I spontaneously explore from that book is called "Erosion."

> *We can tell you our children were born helpless . . . Of their struggle to learn. How they discovered their feet. How they crawled on their knees. How every muscle stretched toward movement. How they listened. How they struggled toward speech.*

I can tell you that every day I struggle toward speech. I surround myself with silence, so that I might hear my sighs. Fill blank pages with my disease? Space with a voice surfacing from sometimes hope and sometimes despair? *Be quiet. You are dead.* Every day I wonder how I will move. *Be still. You are dead.* Every day I stretch, I crawl, toward the future. My muscles are atrophied, but when I fall, I fall forward. *What can you do with your body now? You are dead. You are dead.* Somebody taps me on the shoulder, on my numb flesh, still warm, still chilled and shuddering. Somebody touches me and whispers about my future. I hear and my eyes clear. I hear and I feel my numb legs, take a shaky step. I cry and want to cling to her. Take me with you. Take me into my future. I'm so afraid. She gently moves away and I see that I'm still standing. I am not dead. I cry. I write. I move. I see. I sing. I love. I am not dead. I discover my feet.

> *Suddenly we find that we are no longer straining against all the old conclusions. We are no longer pleading for the right to speak: we have spoken . . .*

Hear me. HEAR ME! My words join and make a new sound. A scream? A love ballad. I shudder. From excitement for the future or from an ice-like memory? But then with these new words, this new language, it shoots up before me: a new land from the ashes of old clichés and foregone conclusions about bodies: my body, my home. I can breathe anew here in this foreign landscape, still unfamiliar but near.

Speak to me. I hear. Hear me. I speak. I shudder. The terrain shifts, leaps, with every utterance of this creation dance.

I never look behind to know what carrion oozes there. As a consequence, I am a new body, shuddering now with a chill yet warm. The ice is melting. It runs its course and drags up debris long buried: silences. I speak and laugh. They laugh and say that I am strong but slipping. I rest here in this foothold: in this body, in these words. And I claim the right. I claim the right to be disintegrating and to call this body, this geography, good. The eroding is the polishing. I have to believe that I shine? Hold me but let me slip away. I am not struggling against all the old conclusions about a body worthy. From my swiftly shifting landscape I shudder, but I can see forever. And so I open my eyes, without blinking. From this location I breathe with a solemn and steady rhythm, and I offer my body to the most brilliant, fiery sunset of my life: my death.

Hold me. Hear me. I shudder and slip away.

> *. . . here language does not contradict what we know.*

I know ecstasy. Listen. I know disease. My voice shakes, but holds. I know where I come from. Let's look behind. Pleasure is my right. I'll tell you my story. I can't see ahead. Hear my hope. Hear my fear. I feel my body coming apart. I speak of pain. I feel my body intact. I feel. Hear my joy.

> *We acknowledge every consequence . . . Weathering (Decay and disintegration). . . . We say that we are part of what is shaped and we are part of what is shaping.*

Hold me up to the light, and you will see that I am decaying. I acknowledge this. And I say that this is terrifying.

"I hope it goes real slow for you." The obese Pain Center nurse with a Betty Boop pin helps to patch my leaky spine and speaks through red lipstick of my future. She wishes me a slow death. Slow.

"You're like all my patients," my neurologist says. "You don't know where your body is in space."

Am I a ghost afraid of death? Is this the consequence of my life? Am I wide-eyed and running out of time, floating among bodies that fall to kiss the ground?

Hold me up to the light, and you will see that I am decaying. How am I a ghost when my toes resemble the soil? And what is speed to toes like soil?

Hold me up to the light, and you will see that I am decaying, part of what is shaped. Disease—my numb feet, my numb calves—makes it so. I acknowledge this. Every time I move, I know that my body is a consequence of disease. I acknowledge this. I am terrified, so I take another step.

Hold me up to the light and you will see that words fill me. Lean in closely and hear me whisper: she says that I am woman, that I know things for this, that I feel things for this, that I am beautiful for this. Words make it so. My mind, my imagination, my body. I am an "abundance of flesh." I hear this. Hear me.

Hold me up to the light and you will see that I am a body full of decay and full of words. My awareness makes this so. With this consequence, these, my words, this, my body, my eroding landscape, I am a part of what is shaping.

> *We sleep and we remember our dreams. We awaken. We tell you we feel every moment; we tell you each detail affects us. We allow ourselves to be overwhelmed. We allow ourselves ecstasy, screaming, hysteria, laughter, weeping, rage, wonder, awe, softness, pain, we are crying out. (There is a roaring inside us, we whisper.) WE ROAR.*

My body becomes the stories I believe about myself.

Storytelling can be a vicious cycle: For example, I was told when young that women were weak, and so I grew up telling myself this same story so often that I forgot the original source. I became the source, and my stories were harmful to my own body.

Mary Daly says that the occasion of a woman acting on her own initiative is mythic since it tells an important story about the power of women. She refers to empowered, storytelling women as "feminist mythmakers."

I love thinking that all of my actions are weaving stories. Living as a woman, I tell others about women. Living as physically challenged, taking my wheelchair around town, I am defining disability. This is a power I never realized I have. I feel the weight and joyful lightness of such responsibility.

New stories are essential for my well-being. I need to be aware of the stories I believe about myself and how they move me. And I am responsible for the stories I tell through my own life and art. They are sure to change as I live, and especially as I connect more with women. But I hope that mine always speak of possibility.

> If I must mimic the posture of the devout, I think I would
> rather go to a mosque for the odd half-hour and cool my head
> on the geometry of complete disinterest, which warns me that
> I had better soon be gone, before the courtyard is white with
> men and fallen angels.
>
> **sara suleri, *meatless days***

A Little Meditation on the Quote

Sara Suleri is referring here to how the Islamic mosque in her city is only open to female worshipers for half an hour per day. I love the image of "cool my head on the geometry of complete disinterest." I imagine her going to the mosque to touch her head to the ground (stone or granite), just as a reminder that organized, even mainstream Islam is not equally inclusive, has less to do with women. I imagine that this gesture would provoke anger, protest, and resolve in her.

I also experienced being erased by organized religion, but within the bosom of evangelical Christianity. At my undergraduate college, a very conservative faction of "Christians" attacked me for being a thinking female. When I led a college work group to build a school in Honduras, some male participants decided once we arrived that they wouldn't listen to anything I said because I was a woman, and women weren't supposed to lead. Soon after, the same group labeled me a heretic because I made assertions about religion that challenged their answers. For example, one day I commented innocently, "The Adam and Eve story is a myth." They hated me for suggesting it.

Sometimes if I sit with devout family members in a church and watch the controlling play of men through the room, I am "cooling my head on the geometry of complete disinterest."

ERINN MAGEE

In this connection someone says jokingly,
tell me your colour and I will tell you who you are.
monique wittig, *les guérillères*

When I first met Erinn she was painting. Sitting Indian-style on a tiled floor, she was bringing to color, to life, brown clay fruit and brown clay Nicaraguan cathedrals. With laughs and flair, she spread color over everything she touched, including me. And although we live countries and cultures apart, she takes personally the color in my life. "Rhonda, I'm afraid of your white walls back in the States. You gotta keep breathing! Color's like oxygen. Don't forget what Nicaragua taught you . . . what I taught you. Where's your yellow, your lavender? Tell me about your orange. I'm worried about your orange. Just a throw pillow will do—and red! If you feel yourself backsliding into earth tones, you're gonna need me face-to-face. Come see me in Panama. Or better yet, I'll visit you in Iowa and bring my paint!"

Embodiment—
understood as rooting
one's identity in the
reality of one's body—
is a principle of many
feminist philosophies.

anita silvers, "disability"

BEING A BEAUTIFUL BODY

> Imagine a world in which every woman is the
> presiding genius of her own body.
>
> **adrienne rich, *of woman born***

Being a body, not *having* a body. The perspective is so simple but revolutionary when truly lived.

I carry with me a comment that recently cracked me open to fuller life. It was a fleeting, seemingly haphazard linguistic statement at first. But it stuck like a paradigm shift, a new language. It felt like a gift, and probably she knew exactly what she was doing.

While we were talking one day, Ellie, a visionary mentor, looked at me head-on and said, "You are a beautiful body." That was it. Nothing more.

I flustered and stammered and didn't know what to say. I was flinching at her words, as they conjured flashbacks of comments referring to the fact that I *have* a beautiful body. In response to her, I think I said something cliché, something like, "Aren't we all really beautiful?"

However, her language felt different, as it caused me immediately to feel my entire body as my identity. It was monumentally body inclusive. Though I'm still not sure of her meaning exactly, I *am* sure of the words' effect on me. I felt happy. I went away asking myself, could she have been talking about my brain? My sensitivity? All of me together? It couldn't have been about physique alone, could it? I loved that I didn't know.

When I returned home, I giddily told Mike about the comment. "She said I was a beautiful body. Isn't that so cool!"

"I've been telling you that for years," he said. "Why didn't you believe *me*?"

"No, no, no!" I protested. "It's *totally* different than saying that I *have* a beautiful body. Don't you see? It's not the same at all!"

But when did I cease thinking I was a beautiful body—a whole, integrated beautiful body? When did I start believing that my physique was the only part of me that could be beautiful, but wasn't the valuable, "real me" at all? It was only something to be controlled and repressed, an enemy that had the god-awful role of representing my worth to the world. How I contorted myself in order to make my narrowly defined body behave in public, so others would think nice things about me. Love me.

When did this debilitating self-hate begin? I didn't dissociate from an identity as an entire body overnight. Dissociation builds over time with enough images, enough comments, and enough dissecting eyes.

Maybe I learned bodily dissociation from men that ogled women on TV. Love and attention, I learned early, is about some kind of fleshy proportion and how my hair fell just so over it all.

What did Randy teach me in Mrs. Cretti's class that time we discussed Plato's allegory of the cave?

He said, "I have an example of one of Plato's forms. Rhonda, could you help me?"

I stand, he points to me and announces, "Rhonda is the form of woman." And he was talking about everything visible. Form!

Then in college, I discovered and lost my breasts at the same time as Meg encouraged me to wear tighter shirts.

"You'll get the guys' attention that way," she said. "They like breasts."

Funny I had never really considered the social role of my breasts before that. But I then understood Randy and male comments to the TV. After Meg's assertion, my breasts seemed to detach from me, becoming a specimen for examination and evaluation beneath a societal magnifier.

I went about my twenties breastless and with a wide-eyed desperation to hang onto my *form*, as if it were truly the last handle to keep me from plummeting into oblivion. Sadly, my maniacal gripping had nothing to do with love, with holding something dearly. Just fear.

With a chopped-up identity, I believed that the *real* me was something internal, like soul, spirit, mind, and all the other words *ad infinitum* that dissect the whole even more. The fleshy body was not the *real* me, I preached. I couldn't escape it, though, despite an earnest go at out-of-body religious ecstasies and the dragging of my physique inhumanely into starvation and other abstinences (sexual), through compulsive exercise, and past mirrors where I only stopped long enough to grimace and turn away in disgust.

The corporeal hate and psychological fragmentation had begun to change for me even before Ellie's comment. I attribute this slow conversion of learning to love myself, of living more fully as a body, to the discipline of body awareness. Ellie's comment complemented what I was already learning and feeling for a year or so, thus encouraging my awareness to snowball.

Now I pause before mirrors to smile and to notice my face and breasts. Oh god, my breasts! Just this last year I discovered those fleshy lumps anew by merely looking down and by *feeling* them as part of me instead of reflecting their image off fashion magazines, or off men, or off other images stored within my unconscious. *I* am beautiful breasts, I realized, beautiful by nature of being breasts, being body. I don't want to misplace them again. When they go, *I* go.

"You are a beautiful body," said Ellie. And I cried afterward, like I have for a year, at the qualitative return—ever closer, ever nearer—of my prodigal self.

MARIA ROSA
Faith

> And we say what he did to her he did to all of us.
> And that one act cannot be separated from another.
>
> **susan griffin, woman and nature**

Balancing a basket of bread on her head, María Rosa usually reached our *colonia* at about 4 p.m., give or take an hour for Nicaraguan "schedules." If I didn't see her coming or yelling, *"¡Pan!"* through the streets and into the houses, she knew I was a regular customer, so would stop and rattle the lock on my iron gate, yelling through our always-opened front door, *"¡Ronda! ¡Doña Ronda!"*

"Buenas tardes, María Rosa," I'd say in greeting, after foraging for spare *Córdobas.* I would meet her out front, unlock the gate, help her lower the heavy basket from atop her head, and consider the daily selection of *pan dulce* and *pan simple,* while engaging in the usual courtesies.

"¿Cómo está, María Rosa?" I'd say.

"Bien, gracias a dios. ¿Y vos?" she'd say back.

"Bien, gracias. ¿Y su familia?" I'd say.

"Como siempre, niños necios."

But children are always getting into some kind of trouble, I'd say while diving into her basket. I liked the braided sweet bread and some of those things shaped like bull's horns—oh, and for Mike, that funny *pan dulce* with unidentified pink oozy stuff.

María Rosa was only one of a daily stream of vendors with odds and ends on their backs and heads, who yelled their wares and services through the streets. We could buy most anything without ever leaving our tiny house—even toilet paper. Our *colonia* was quiet and secluded within an already small *San Marcos.* Being the only foreigners in the area, our address was *"La Colonia Manuel Moya; los gringos."* Anyone in town could find us with that much information. And if a random *gringo o gringa* came looking for us when we weren't home, most anyone along the street was happy to offer what time we left and in which direction we were walking. Eyes and gossip were everywhere, but our neighbors looked out for us, even though many thought me a witch—but a good one! Why else, they whispered to one another, would I fill the house with candles at night?

I knew María Rosa better than the rest of the vendors since she was Karla's sister. Karla was our *empleada;* but more than scrubber of our floors and undies, she was my friend and personal Nicaraguan cultural prophet. I would sometimes pull up a plastic bucket seat to where she wrestled our laundry by hand at the outdoor water basin and let the Nica-oracle field my endless whys and *por qués*—mostly dealing with Nicaraguan men and women.

One day I had her teach me the Spanish word for "castrate" and "castration," the verb and noun both, not surprised at all that they were English cognates. Afterward, I practiced using them in a sentence—in the spirit of language acquisition, of course.

"Hay que castrar todos los hombres Nicaragüenses."

"Aveces la castración es la buena."

"Hoy, castramos todo el pueblo."

"Karla, ¿quien quiere Ud. castrar?"

"¡Qué barbaridad!" Karla would always say to my forward *gringa* ways, while laughing.

Karla knew that I absolutely hated her defense of Nicaraguan men when she claimed, that's just the way they are.

"Así son los hombres Nicaragüenses," she'd say.

That was her comment after María Rosa came by one day carrying facial bruises with her *pan.* I couldn't believe that she ho-hummed her sister's abuse as the way of Nicaraguan men—as if they themselves were victims of biology. Karla told me that María Rosa's unemployed husband was very verbally and physically violent to his wife and kids. She assured me that the family was trying to help, but things were *"muy complicados en Nicaragua."*

"Así son los hombres Nicaragüenses."

The only complication I saw was that many Nicaraguan men were both assholes and "spiritual leaders." They seemed to grow like some kind of tropical killer fungus through women's bodies, no matter how much the women bartered, prayed, and "sold their souls" to support them. They might beat their wives and fuck around, but they really can't help themselves, the *pobrecitos!*

"Así son los hombres Nicaragüenses."

Whenever María Rosa came by, I always paid close attention to her health, wondering what to do and when to do it—my normal internal battle while living smack dab within the poorest country in the entire Western Hemisphere—after Haiti. Women's shelters were beginning to sprout up in Managua and other larger cities, but husbands still had legal and "sacred" rights over the bodies of their wives and kids. *Complicado, sí.*

For a while, María Rosa didn't have bruises, until the day she bopped by, well-battered but looking like she might explode with confidence and strength.

"¿Cómo está?" I asked her, worried.

"¡Ay, bien, bien! ¡Gracias a dios!"

I'm not sure why, but over the course of our transactions she always told me as much about herself as she could. This time she gushed the good news of how she had just written a letter to Cristina and had faith that Cristina would surely answer, that Cristina was going to rescue her and her children. She asked me, wouldn't Cristina help? And she asked me, wouldn't Cristina find them a new home away from *el abuso?* And María Rosa was so intently fixing my eyes with hers.

Emotions of all sorts went crashing through me, since I suspected who Cristina was —I had lived in Latin America long enough. But I didn't want to deflate her by asking for sure. I just stared into her bruised face and her determined look that waited for the "authoritative" *gringa* response. *My* response. Basically, she wanted me to assure her that a god existed.

"Hay que esperar, María Rosa. Hay que esperar," I said. She left, happy, and I returned inside, frustrated and raging to myself, who am I to talk about hope here? Here?

Although I was alarmingly sure of her identity, I wanted to verify my horror about Cristina.

"Karla, ¿quien es Cristina?" I asked. *"¿Ella de quien habla María Rosa?"*

When Karla wondered if I referred to the *Latina* talk show host, I pulled up a bucket and cried.

María Rosa still came by daily with warm bread—sometimes a sewing machine— but she never mentioned Cristina again. Usually she wasn't bruised, but sometimes she was. Always I saw her. Always I acknowledged her pain to myself. Always . . . eventually . . . I turned away so she wouldn't confuse my face with Cristina's.

III

BODIES IN FOCUS
A Photography Project of Seeing Women

We photograph

what we love

to see.

ellie epp

NATURE PHOTOGRAPHY DREAM

Dream

I'm in a large room full of women: reclining women, women leaning in nooks, women kicking back in chairs. They all look strong. It's how they hold their bodies. It's how they dress. It's in their faces.

We are meeting prior to going on a nature photography fieldtrip. Somebody asks about my photography work of the past. I address the room. My explanation is followed with a question of why I, with my physical challenges, want to join them on a nature photography fieldtrip.

I answer, "To photograph all of you."

Dream Meditation

I never thought I would do nature photography again. I was wrong.

Prior to the dream I read Susan Griffin's book, *Woman and Nature: The Roaring Inside Her.* Prior to the dream I cried about how my physical disabilities separate me from intimacy with mountains and trees and rivers and dirt. Prior to the dream I asked myself how I could possibly reincorporate photography into my life considering my new physical limitations.

Women in nature is the answer.

To photograph women is to commune intensely with nature is to realize my vocation. How can I talk only of what I have lost to disease?

Timed Freewrite to the Dream

I'm standing in a room with women. They don't understand why I'm with them, when I'm not capable. Nature photography! Nature photography? But I can, I tell them, see I can go with you and have a different sort of nature in my viewfinder: You. You are nature, don't you see? You are the most beautiful sort. Why mountains, rivers, trees, why the way the sun hits that flower? Why all that other nature when I can know you with my eyes, my whole body, my camera? I can't connect in the same way with rocks and lakes. They can't move through me like you can, like my blood, my own flesh. I can show the world your beauty, the beauty I'm mute to describe, so let's only look as your shoulder dips in the dusk and your neck tilts. Please don't hide yourself! I won't hurt you. I just want to know you in a place of discomfort and make it safe and make it light and make it like beauty and like ease and like hope and like rest and like where we live. Let's explore one another's eyes.

I see you.

SEEING WOMEN
Imaging My Passion

My darkroom is light tight. I slip a white sheet of paper into a tray of developer solution. I lift an edge of the tray and ease the solution back and forth across it. The movement is key if I want something to happen. I continue this motion while marking the time on a large, square, glow-in-the-dark clock with a monstrous hand circling the seconds. After about thirty seconds, by the red hue of my safelight, I see tonal movement across the paper. Black lines and spots begin to appear like smudges. With more seconds, the smudges become shapes. With more seconds, the shapes join and fill in with more and more detail.

I gasp as I recognize the shape of a woman—a naked woman. I knew this image would appear as I had just seen the negative. I knew her form as latent in the paper. But it still surprises me when she becomes an enlarged positive. I hear and feel myself breathing through the seconds that ease the paper through to the solution that fixes her image.

With the passing of enough breath, I turn on the white light and see the woman across the paper. My heart leaps even more as I get this better look at the visual integrity of her body. Does my body respond with passion because it remembers the intimate process of photographing her? Does it leap because, in seeing the image on the paper,

I feel my own body more acutely for how it is visually similar? In other words, does my passion result from feeling intensely female?

Even after her image is fixed on the paper, I'm not finished with my attentions. I will wash it once, soak it in a solution of photographic soap, and wash it again in a fish tank-looking machine that rinses it for archival preservation. I will lay the 11x14 sheets of clean, exhibition-quality paper on contamination-free drying screens until they wrinkle up as a result of the total dissipation of moisture. At this point I will move them one by one through a Community Center heat press to make them flat, mail them to a professional retoucher, get them back with dust spots and random smudges fully cleaned up, and then store them until I matte and frame for exhibit.

However, I don't just store the portraits in an archival box. I have spent so much attentive time with the images that I store them also within my own body. They join the words and images of other women to inform my emotional, physical, and intellectual movement, provoking this new passion I have for living. How can I possibly live well without awareness of how I join and belong? My darkroom is full of light because of how I newly see women and see myself.

I love to see women. I am imaging my passion.

The photography project began with my third semester residency at Goddard College—actually before that if fear is foreplay for creation. A residency is eight full days spent in a community of students and faculty from around the world who descend all at once on Plainfield, Vermont, for encouraging hugs, enlightening conversations, mind- and body-expanding workshops, and motivational kicks in the ass, or "gentle nudges." After the time there, we all return home to begin our very individual semester and life work. It's an exhausting time, but for me it's like the truest sort of homecoming, or a dream vacation. I feel safe, accepted, and free to risk and abandon myself to living—with support. I can't sleep the night before I leave. And I'm so excited once I get there and see that I'm not alone, that I almost never want to close my eyes for fear that the place might leave in the night. At Goddard I expose myself.

I stood over my suitcase before leaving for the residency that August, wondering what to do with my camera. A photography project idea kept popping up in my brain like a damn nuisance. But doing it just wouldn't be safe.

"Photographing women is your way of returning photography and nature to your life," my dream had told me.

"That's wonderful," my classmate Carolyn agreed. "Portraits of nude women . . . and writing. That's your work . . . your body work!"

I stood over my suitcase then, that August, wondering what to do with my camera. I would take it with me to the residency—that was a given. I had made an oath to myself about it earlier in the summer. I "crossed my heart hoped to die" that no matter how I felt when I stood over my suitcase before the next residency, I would take my camera . . . in case . . . just in case I felt like using it . . . in some way . . . but I really wasn't committing.

My question as I stood over my suitcase was not whether or not my camera would go with me. I wondered where to pack it. I had never before in my photography life beginning at age twelve, checked it in a suitcase. Never! It was too precious not to travel in my carry-on, close to my body.

But as I stood over my suitcase, I felt no sentiment for my camera. I had to buy the Nikon N90 as I began to lose my eyesight, as disease messed with my vocation. It wasn't my fully manual, fully do-it-myself Nikon FM2, which was like family. After college I backpacked around parts of Asia, Africa, and Central America with it. I took it down the Nile and up into the Himalayas. I wandered for hour after sweaty hour with it: along beaches, dirt trails, and animal carcass-strewn alleys; through rice and kelp fields, Indian monsoons, Egyptian pyramids, and Palestinian refugee camps. With joy and determination, my camera and I sought out hidden away, foreign bodies. I have never seen so many faces so well. They burned for the seeing. I burned for the seeing. We connected, despite skin color and language barriers. My portraits imaged my passion. I had left the States, hoping to "find myself." I returned home a portrait photographer.

My FM2 was my comrade in passion, but since it didn't automatically make my world come into focus, I gave it up for the N90. From the first day I bought it, I always considered askance my N90, never head-on like a friend. It was an impersonal machine with digital readouts, buttons, and mirrors—sometimes beeps. It reminded me all too blatantly that I couldn't see well. Then when I lost my eyesight *almost* completely, and my portrait business most definitely, it reminded me that I couldn't see at all—that I was dying.

I was thirty when I lost my eyesight. My blindness was called "legal," and MS and eye specialists guessed that I wouldn't see again. Imagine how I felt while sitting outside Fido coffee shop one day, thinking I saw red on a far building. For two years I had seen only light, shadow, and yellow. Then hunched over my latte, I was swept to new consciousness by green and red and blue and bricks and doors and light posts and sidewalks with cracks, and . . . and . . . and . . . Imagine how I cried.

Maybe I blame my N90 for my lameness. Starting with the latte incident, my eyesight had returned enough to use autofocus again. Mike and I moved to Nicaragua so he could teach and I could have a go at both adventure and my old photographic ways. Almost as soon as I arrived, my legs, which never gave me any trouble before that, wouldn't carry me like they used to. I started using a cane, I began taking bicycle taxis around an already-tiny town, we moved to a house three blocks closer to our friends and to our bar and eatery hangout. Because my photography style was active, I gave it up altogether. I chose despair.

I stood over my suitcase then, that August before the residency, wondering if I dared. I dared. I packed over $2,000 of uninsured photographic equipment among my clothing, wrapped up in my socks and underwear. If it got lost, I thought, that was really no problem. I didn't much care since I wasn't even sure why I was taking it to the residency in the first place—other than the cross my heart promise two months earlier. Residencies are exhausting for me.

"Think of it like this," an MS nurse told me. "You have a step quota. You can take only so many in one day before your body won't budge. You might think about planning your time with this in mind."

I unpacked as soon as I arrived at Goddard after a marathon day of travel: being rushed madly in an airport wheelchair to my connection, asking strangers to help load me with my backpack, taking off my leg brace for the x-ray machine, putting my cane through too, getting wide-eyed and planning for escape and cover-up as my bladder filled and I couldn't use a toilet immediately, popping anti-fatigue drugs, meeting fellow traveling students in Chicago, feeling like I was closer and closer to home.

I unpacked, but my legs stopped participating. Did I surpass my step quota already, I wondered? I can't really gauge my fatigue with the nurse's precision since my body just stops and starts whimsically. I only have a few controls: rest and stimulants. I rested on my bed, unpacked a little, rested some more, popped a pill, unpacked . . .

I saw only trees from my room's window. The desk lamp was old, with a funky shade. I felt cozy. My camera. It made it. Nobody stole it, although I saw the suitcase was opened. At first I thought I forgot a lens, and then found it in a sock, rolled under the bed.

I could hardly straighten my back and legs as I meticulously situated my photographic things in the bureau, one drawer for my camera and lenses; one for film, brushes, and other cleaners; one for my portfolio from . . . before. I saw only trees from my room's window. The desk lamp was huge, with blue and white flowers on the shade. A mirror was leaning against the closet wall. I liked the room light. I could barely stand.

Before Goddard I never really saw women very well. I could more or less expertly pick out body parts in a crowd, but I didn't really acknowledge their unique intelligence or sexuality, or myself experience the world from a female perspective. In short, I didn't see whole bodies. How could I have, when I didn't see or know my whole self either? I call this blind, psychologically dissociated time my "ghost years."

Maybe my family first taught me not to see women. My parents didn't seem to notice my developing body. Not outwardly, anyway. Their embarrassment at my bodily changes, if their silence was due to unease, fueled my own discomfort with my changing body.

Their silence suggested a not-seeing. For all of us I didn't menstruate, my breasts didn't grow, and my emotions were not so important. To their sight and mine, then, I was not at all an integrated body. Did their dissociation encourage my own? I questioned most everything my family did or believed but never from the perspective of being female—from my own body. Did I ever really know anything?

I'm not sure why I decided to do the photography project. Had I stared at my camera enough that I remembered something important to my body? Something like an awareness practice that made me so focused, happy, and excited as I sought out faces? Had my reading of feminist literature and feminist theory compelled me to see women and myself so newly and intensely that expressing my transformed perspective was natural and necessary? Both, I think: I was reclaiming my vocation and my female identity.

Therefore, Friday morning, the first full day of that residency in August, I photographed Anne naked.

Anne picked me up in her red Toyota truck out back of Kilpatrick dorm. The sun had recently risen, and I felt exhilarated and nervous about what we were planning. I had gotten up over an hour earlier, when it was still dark, since my body needs to ease into movement. I rotated in my bed, set both legs on the floor, and then slowly put weight on them to test that they would support the rest of me. They were okay that day. Excitement.

I continued my morning ritual of waking: cold water to the face, green tea, and an anti-fatigue pill. Though they wouldn't help in waking me, I also popped an incontinence drug. I needed a social bladder for a few days. After about 45 minutes of these attentions, my legs grew sturdier, my eyes saw more clearly, my MS morning brain fog subsided, and I felt much more present in my body: aware and confident about how I planned to move.

When I climbed into her truck, I wanted Anne to choose our spot. She knew of a private field. We drove a little, turned a few times, went down a dirt road, stopped. Excitement. She was a little sleepy.

The field was perfect, with its tall grass and white-capped flowers—or weeds. I immediately saw what I needed to do with Anne. Usually I get a quick, intuitive sense of how an environment will complement or reveal my subject. If it isn't really fitting, I improvise. The confidence makes me feel like a photographer—a seer.

The morning was moist and misty—not cold, but I wasn't the one stripping. I told Anne I was ready. She took off her clothes, slowly, with meditatively smooth motions. Neither of us felt awkward, I think. It was such a natural thing for her to be doing there in that damp morning. It was natural for me too, to be there with her, seeing her with enough attention and respect to want to document her body in that space and time.

I began . . .

I directed her into the field and pictured her in the center of natural space. I try not to pose a subject other than just enough to illuminate her with nice light and to make her feel comfortable. I felt happy there in the field, seeing Anne. But after a few exposed frames, I stopped and dropped the camera from my eye. Something wasn't quite right about my angle of view.

"I need to see you from a higher perspective," I said. She backed her truck ten feet, dropped the tailgate, and I climbed up. Yes, I was where I needed to be.

After taking some shots from the tailgate, I hopped down to her level again, and we moved for a while through the field. I took some pictures of her from closer up, but never so close that I didn't surround her with nature. I wanted to photograph her *whole* body. When I claimed, "that's enough," Anne dressed again with the same, meditative attention, we backtracked down the dirt road, turned a little, drove some more, arrived at Kilpatrick dorm, stopped, and separated with "see you later."

My heart was pounding, and my face must have been brilliant then. I sat on my bed, remembering back to the field and to Anne and me all there together. I felt so alive, so passionate. My morning's awareness ritual was more complete than ever.

My time with Anne set the tone for my week of seeing women. I met with others in the early morning or right before dusk, but sometimes we'd sneak off in the afternoon between workshops and meetings, looking for shade or bright window light. My week's attention was on light and women (Can I even separate?). I was so happy.

Each session was highly individual—one on one. She would come by my room where I had already been sitting and breathing for a while, building strength. I could see trees out my window. Loved my lampshade! I cleaned my lenses every morning. My camera. When she arrived, I would sit with her a moment in order to calm us both.

Where would we go, I wondered? How much nakedness, if any?

As we left, I asked her to carry my backpack, to help me, and I explained matter-of-factly that my body might collapse without warning. I didn't want to surprise or scare her.

"It doesn't hurt me," I assured.

Whenever we went out together, it felt a little dangerous. Of course, there was the exciting element of secret nakedness on a college campus. But each time, I also felt the exhilaration of leaping into the unknown. I didn't know when and where my body might stop. Risky, but so much fun. I was on a new sort of adventure.

"Did you know, Rhonda, that when you have a camera in your hands, your body looks strong? You hardly limp, and you climb all over everything!"

I kept hearing comments to this effect all week and thought of the paradox: When I photograph women I feel my body very intensely, but I also forget multiple sclerosis for those minutes of intimate communion. Maybe integrating a new and former passion was the best treatment for my disease.

Residencies are exhausting for me. That August I attended the regularly scheduled events, but I also met with and photographed attentively fourteen women, all in different stages of nakedness (with the right attention, even a clothed portrait is about exposure). It seems that I radically surpassed my step quota during that week, but health theories seem silly with enough passion leading my body.

I stood over my suitcase then, at the end of that August residency. I wondered what to do with my camera. I began to stuff it into clothing like before, then stopped. It didn't seem right to me, and I knew exactly what to do about it. I gathered up my photographic equipment from the suitcase and arranged it thoughtfully in my carry-on. My camera!

It wasn't like all the women were itching to expose themselves, and that's the beauty of my project. It was a tough decision for many of them, some taking all week to get up the nerve. But when they decided "why the hell not!" the one-on-one session was so freeing for both of us. I'm not sure how to describe how they opened. I just saw release seem to leap from their bodies. Could have been how they breathed differently. Could have been how they let their arms and shoulders relax after time.

When I told people later that I'm doing a project of photographing women—most of them naked—they usually responded, "How did you find them? Did you put an ad in the paper?"

God, the question provoked me. I realized I was offended because the one asking didn't comprehend the magnitude or purpose of my project. I was offended because I take women's bodies personally now. I want all female bodies to be seen. And I want the woman I see attentively enough to photograph to feel valued as a body and to feel herself more intensely as a result. I'm energized by the connection that results from seeing the bodies of other women. It's a body dialogue that leads to self-knowledge and well-being.

Many people in this society think that a body worthy of being exposed, or seen with respect, has to be a certain kind of body. I was formerly guilty of this thinking enough to hate and hide my own body for a long time. People assume that a body that I choose to photograph or a body that wants to be photographed in the first place, is a body that conforms to the "rules."

Because of my disgust at "innocent" comments about my process of photographing women, I understand my purpose much better: I photographed female bodies for the simple and profound reason that they were female bodies, therefore immeasurably worthy of being seen well and valued. I'm so happy that I listened to my body impelling me forward into the project without having it all theoretically figured out beforehand.

The project reincorporated a former passion into my life—portrait photography. I used it to follow a newly discovered passion—seeing and valuing women—and I realized that disease doesn't at all exclude passion from my life's work and dreams. My exhibit will depict this harmonic convergence through my body that helped me see women profoundly enough to celebrate my visual and ontological transformation.

Even if I go blind again or disease prohibits photography later, I *feel* my body more for having done this project, and I hope that the portrait subjects and other women who see the exhibit feel theirs differently as well.

I photograph exposed women. I love to see women. I am imaging my passion.

SEEING

Quoted from Laura Sewall's *Sight and Sensibility*

[Perception is a] mutual interaction, an intercourse, coition, so to speak, of my body with things.
david abram

My eyes are the earth gazing at itself.
richard nelson

We are the landscape of all we have seen.
isamu noguchi

Where there is not vision, the people perish.
proverbs 29:18

PICTURING WOMEN

. . . she sees suddenly that her legs are woman's legs. Her shoulders drop softly and infinitely. Her belly rounds into dark hair. She is moved to call herself beautiful, to see the abundance of her skin . . .

susan griffin, woman and nature

I never imagined that so many would strip. I never expected that they would take off their clothes for my camera, for me.

I told them they could if they wanted to . . . but only if they wanted to . . . to strip. "Just for you," I said. "Nobody else has to see." "Only if you feel comfortable enough." "But wouldn't it be nice?"

So many exposed women. One place. One week. One.

For me each session was like a meditation. Attention. One person at a time only. Vital. Just one, or it became noisy and not so much about us and how we moved together.

"What makes a good portrait?" some ask.

Breath.

I would begin each session by breathing before we met, whether early morning or evening.

Inhale . . .

With hushed morning tones we chatted, we subjects, on the way to a spot worthy enough to contain us—the forest usually. We talked more concretely of the upcoming shoot. What did she want? Where would we go? And I would sometimes have to breathe for her.

Exhale . . .

Upon arrival at our destination, slowly I would move and spin to notice light and how it fell on her, background and how it accompanied her, foreground and how it hid and exposed, camera settings and how they helped it all, and anything else that would express her, express us.

Inhale . . .

If she wanted to feel her body uncovered, comfort with this kind of exposure took more time for some, and less for others. But remembering that rhythm depends on the space in between, we rested when we needed to.

Exhale . . .

I would attend to our breath in flashes as the time unfolded, breathing through tight-ness and inflexibility.

"What do you want me to do?" most would ask, not sure where to put her hands, how to hang her arms. "Tell me what you want."

Feel yourself move. Just Feel.

Inhale . . .

I was aware when my eyes were not attentive to the woman before me.

Breathe . . .

I could feel when too much of a focus on line and shape and f-stops and film burning made her start to disappear before me.

Breathe . . . and breathe . . .

Most sessions were quiet and about the presence of bodies: hers and mine. Bodies:

ours. I was present enough to forget all that wasn't before me. She was present enough to forget what stood in the way. And we were both present enough to forget the rest of the campus as we danced our way toward integration.

Anne was my first since I knew her already, knew she was open, knew that I myself needed to get used to such a new rhythm between women. I don't think she saw how I transfigured there, breathing in and out, in and out, there in the tall grass that flew up between us, sometimes revealing, sometimes hiding. I need a new perspective, I thought then: A higher angle. So I crawled onto her truck's tailgate and forgot. I forgot my legs, forgot I couldn't. Forgot.

See how Debbie laughs nervously, calls me crazy, and says with light in her eyes, "I'll take it all off, but just skin. No breasts or crotch. Just skin. Only skin."

Vivi's body is not so much her own yet. I saw that. I saw her eyes leave and float somewhere beyond, behind me, ripped from their sockets, I think, by a life of high fashion, of modeling body alienation.

"One good picture terrified me," she said. "I worried that in the next I would be too fat, too old, too freckled. You know what I mean. Not good enough."

I knew what she meant.

Andi hates everything above her neck.

"Not my face," she said. "I don't like my face at all—or my brain, but that won't show up on film."

I didn't tell her that it all shows up.

I respected her self-loathing and photographed her nude silhouette. But I regret it. I regret that I pictured her as a shadow.

Lise sees right through me. I felt uncomfortably naked around her, having already exposed myself to her through writing.

"I'm not going to take my clothes off," she said as we ducked into the trees. She heard the rumor.

"I wasn't expecting you to," I said.

We both felt awkward. I could tell this as I stood there exposed, noticing how the light fell through her skin too.

Carol and I locked ourselves in an upstairs bathroom with nice window light, and we wonder still that nobody tried the handle.

"Just my breasts and necklace," she said.

Carol Scott, named for her dead grandfather—and dead brother—Scott. Both dead. But laughing breasty in a lighted corner by the toilet. Alive.

Carolyn has breast issues.

"Boys always made fun of them," she said. "Girls too."

Carolyn didn't want to get wet or dirty and theorized beforehand about easing into nakedness, exposing her crotch first. Carolyn with her breasts and her ideas, losing all her clothes at once, flying her arms in the air and thrusting her body forward to say, "Look at me! Look at me!"

I looked.

I could hardly hear quiet Christine say okay to a portrait, could hardly hear that she wanted to wear clothing, could hardly hear much of what she mumbled. But I felt she really wanted to, felt that she might someday speak louder—yell maybe.

Emily stripped in the trees with such attention that I could see her feeling it, see her knowing something new. Was it air? Skin? Relationship? Was it the integrity of being a beautiful body there with nature, there among her own?

Melissa, Favor, and I swam naked at the quarry . . . in the early morning . . . with the haze. We photographed one another half on land, half in water. Morning breathed across our bodies, tiptoeing over sharp rocks and squishing through soft mud to rest in the ease of water, and nudity, and connection. The haze cleared as we went on.

Anne photographed me in a field of flowers.

"No, they're weeds," she laughed.

Beautiful nevertheless, I thought, when seen up close without the cover-up of a name. I felt beautiful too, without clothes, without symbols, for the simple reason that

I was standing naked in a field of white and green things shooting up around me.

Jeanne was my last and thanked me for asking, for taking the time for her. Earlier in the week, she wore clothes for a session. Later she wore none. In the meditation room, she wore none. In the trees, she wore none. Exposed.

"Do you realize what you are doing for women here?" she said to me throughout the week.

Did they realize what they did for me?

"What does embodiment feel like?" Lise asked me.

Like I felt when picturing women. Passion. Connection. Joy.

BODIES IN FOCUS

The *Bodies in Focus* exhibit and PowerPoint presentation are my movement to get the images into the world. The goal of our communal time is to begin to fall deeper in love with being alive: with being a body.

Bodies in Focus is a tribute to women, as well as a safe place for most women to be themselves bravely and shamelessly. The photographic exhibit does not feature all varieties of women. Rather, it shares my intimate look at a few friends and acquaintances who surrounded me in a low-residency Goddard College setting over two one-week periods in August 2003 and January 2004. I later added to the exhibit a portrait of my sweet and body-loving 90-year-old grandma.

I began the project out of anger at body privilege, anger that most of the cultural images I see of women—especially in advertising and the entertainment media—feature the same general kind of body: a fallacious prototype! Believing that not seeing is not valuing, I worked passionately to photograph—to see—just a few real women. My photographs naturally counter female-harmful cultural opinions and pressures about beauty and worth. But my process of photographing was itself vital to the larger project. In addition to proving that I valued each woman enough to photograph her so attentively, I also offered my subjects and me a new, intense, and transformational experience as bodies.

When word got around that my project involved photographing exposure, most often nakedness, the idea of posing naked was scary for most women and unthinkable for some. The women saw me approach and raised their hands, fearing my impending question. I tried to put them at ease: "May I photograph you? I would photograph any form of nakedness. If you only want to show your face I would consider that exposure." Most of them have never posed naked. That is so important to me: the women didn't approach me, I approached them, and asked them to expose themselves. Everybody I asked eventually took advantage of the unique and daring opportunity for exposure— and enjoyed it!

I met privately with each. We were always alone together, without onlookers. The student and I met in a place of her choice, whether in woods, fields of weeds or snow, dorm rooms, or prayer rooms. She decided how much of herself to expose, and then we moved together as I worked to reveal her with light. I never posed them, just let it happen.

While talking with the women during our sessions, I realized my greater purpose: we were addressing their body "scars." Many have suffered from some kind of trauma, and by photographing them I was aiding in their recovery from eating disorders, substance abuse, physical abuse, religious repression, and overall alienation from their bodies.

I printed all images of my choosing. I sent each woman photocopies of her images and asked for a five-minute written response to her portrait. The photograph and the response were both vital aspects of my project. I framed them in 16-inch by 20-inch frames and exhibited them in a room with all the images surrounding the viewer. For my graduation presentation, I read from one of my writings, and each woman read her written reflections out loud in the room where the portraits were displayed.

The *Bodies in Focus* exhibit and presentation is a venue for the photographed women to share their body images, as well as their written meditations on either the process of being photographed or on seeing the final portrait for the first time. They believe themselves to be body activists, advocates for all female bodies, whether like their own or not. We hope that the brave exposure will encourage viewers to think differently about bodies: about their own and about others.

We all need their bodies.

PORTRAITS

I photographed Kate also naked but she wanted a clothed picture on display, since lots of her family members would be seeing the exhibit up on the walls with other portraits. She didn't want to "come out" to her family members and her boyfriend's family in such a stark way.

"... my nakedness seems completely natural and necessary."

Kate

Christine did not share any written words with me, but her photo session seemed to make her scream to the outside world, "I am here." Our photo session was very personal, but out of my own shyness I did not ask her to disrobe. I think I read in her posture that I would only photograph her face.

I always tell the women that a portrait of only the face is also an important aspect of exposure.

Christine

Carol waited until the end of the residency to decide to go naked. Halfway between workshops she grabbed me and said, "I want to do it." So in a bathroom—toilet in the background—she exposed only her breasts.

"My face, breasts and stance depict a life lived fully, from the sag of the breasts from childbirth, the facial lines and . . . I'm starting to cry . . . I just really like the woman I see in this picture—I acknowledge myself in a way I don't think I ever have before.

"It was a very freeing moment for me . . . a wonderful opportunity to experience my body in a totally new way . . . [It] comes at an incredibly important time in my life when I'm trying to settle into my aging body like I've never been in my body before . . . I still feel inside my head like that child struggling to understand what being a woman means, and what I see in this photograph is someone who already knows. I have a whole different feeling about myself now . . . This photo is a gift and a testimony to myself . . ."

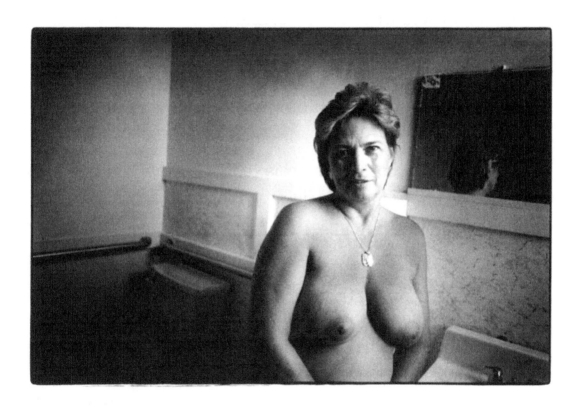

Carol

Lise saw right through me. I felt uncomfortably naked around her, having already exposed myself to her through writing.

"I'm not going to take my clothes off," she said as we ducked into the trees. She heard the rumor.

"I wasn't expecting you to," I said.

We both felt awkward. I could tell this as I stood there exposed, noticing how the light fell through her skin too.

"I am almost never relaxed when my photo is being taken. I feel something is being expected of me, at the very least a smile. It wasn't like that with Rhonda. She had such authority as a photographer. I felt she knew just exactly what she wanted in this session, and what she wanted had nothing to do with my smiling. Knowing this allowed me to relax, to drop down into myself. I don't remember whose idea it was for me to have my back against a tree, but that helped too. This portrait captures an essence I don't think any other photo of me ever has. In the years since it was taken I have had several profound experiences leaning back against a tree so it also feels like a photo with a memory of the future."

Lise

Anne was my first portrait subject. I photographed her originally in different areas, but nothing seemed quite right. I surveyed the scene and wanted to express her connection to nature.

> "My body is present . . . [My] face doesn't seem as embodied as my body . . . I think you have captured me exceptionally well, particularly the part of me that feels strong, capable, a little hard. I have never had an image of myself that feels as real."

Anne

Jeanne is a hoot. I photographed her both outside on the grass and inside, and this prayer space appealed to my aesthetic sensibilities because of the chipping paint and nice window light.

"... I stood there, asking what to do with my hands and which way you wanted me to look and how should I stand, busying myself with the obvious physicalities, but inside, my spirit stood with arms outstretched, face turned upward, and frolicked like a wind-blown leaf on the unobstructed, freshly mowed lawn."

Jeanne

Everybody I talked to at the residency couldn't believe that Debbie was going to participate in my "exposure" project. She did, stipulating that this naked photographer could not see her naked.

"On viewing this picture and seeing myself in a different way, I began to consider that I should see myself more compassionately."

Debbie

Emily loved being naked. As she strolled through the trees, she was light and turned in circles as if she were reaching out to touch the environment around her.

She chose to be photographed topless, crossing her arms around her breasts. Later I said to her, "Emily, you still have a nipple sticking out." And she answered, "No matter, just a little peek-a-boob."

> "I was actually cognizant enough to sleep without my underwear . . . I was like, note to self: Do not wear underwear the night before you do pictures with Rhonda as it leaves pink lines in your thigh fat.
>
> "I'm standing behind [Rhonda] while she fiddles with the key to her room . . . People walk past us. I have this sneaky feeling that nobody knows what we were just up to—like we just had sex or something. It feels that secretive and intimate to me . . . It feels like being really awake."

Emily

I met Cyndi in our adviser Ellie Epp's small group meeting, which was for helping us all with our writing projects. Cyndi is alluring. Not because of her way cool black lab help dog or because of her writing plans. Cyndi is really sweet. She knew I had been taking a lot of portraits, and was quick to volunteer for a session.

At the group, Cyndi spoke urgently about wanting to write about her estranged family. She wondered if any of us had new angles for her approach. She was urgent, not knowing that she would die. Or did she? Thinking back on it now, I wonder whether she knew she was seriously ill. Is that why she had a help dog?

I can't help but cry to myself. What happened to Cyndi? Was she able to complete her very important writing work before she died of pancreatic cancer? And what about her help dog? Is she helping somebody else? Has she been helping other people who have died like Cyndi? What toll has that had on her childlike approach to other humans? Has the writing of this snippet given me the distance I need from Cyndi's reality?

Cyndi

I photographed Melissa naked at a steamy quarry lake with Favor. Despite my interest in nakedness, I chose this head shot because I was drawn by the intensity of her face. It felt like her.

I received no response to this portrait, but I hear that Melissa didn't like it. Her stare is so powerful and penetrating. I said to her, "Melissa, that is who you are."

Melissa

I photographed everybody's face, but Favor was very solitary during that residency. So solitary that I did not want to disrupt and encourage her to look up. By the next residency, she told me that she was in a different place and would now look up at my camera/me.

> In this time
> of abundance,
> odd
> that she should be
> so hungry.

Favor

Carolyn has always had boob issues. Girls and boys, men and women have always brought up the issue of her large breasts and teeny tiny frame. So as Carolyn and I searched out the spot where she wanted to be photographed, she asked me to only photograph her crotch. The crotch was safe. Photographing her boobs would be painful for her. I told her that I do head shots, but not crotch shots. So after that discussion, she stripped, threw her arms in the air, as if to say, "Look at me!"

"The first time I looked at the photos, a voice inside my head said, 'God, you're ugly.' But that is the old story . . . I went out to buy a magnifying glass to prove that [the voice] was wrong. I inspected the [contact sheets] then like a scientist or researcher looking for clues that my body had some redeeming qualities . . . [In] the photos where I am clowning around, there is a . . . joyous light quality. That light is who I really am. It's seeping out of every curve, every pore . . . I want to tell that voice inside me that is saying, 'God, you're ugly' to SHUT THE FUCK UP! I'm gorgeous."

Carolyn

Andi specifically didn't want me to photograph her face. People, men and women, have always responded positively to her body, but not to her face. I think that this picture is beautiful, but the loss of her face makes the experience incomplete. Her photograph becomes a nude rather than a naked one.

According to John Burger's definition, "To be nude is to be seen naked by others and yet not recognized for oneself . . . To be naked is to be without disguise . . . A naked body has to be seen as an object in order to become a nude."

Reading Andi's words, I wonder why she feels that her body does not reflect the fire of her personality. What would that fire look like?

". . . the fire I feel inside is invisible in the body."

Andi

Ana and I are directly by a dorm. One guy woke up, looked out the window and said to himself, "Is that a naked woman in that field?" Then he turned around, saying to himself, "Cool."

Since Ana is Colombian, she was not accustomed to snow. She wanted to wear boots in some snowy field somewhere. So we took a few steps away from our dorm. I could tell she was so excited.

"I write different versions of what I feel, and deep down I have the feeling that nothing I've written is frank enough: They are all versions, versions of a woman's insecurity about her body. Masks. It is like, unless I make a story for this, unless I surround this image with my words, make it mine, I will not be able to deal with the fact that I am there, in the middle of a Vermont forest, knee deep in the snow, naked and grinning.

"I want to thank you for the experience, Rhonda . . . for putting us at the edge with ourselves."

Ana

Lisa has no words to match this picture, this experience, but she did talk to me about her study focus. She hoped to work with Lise, to write a novel. It would be a novel about two lesbians. I don't know what she ended up with.

Lisa

Vivi wanted to leave behind her modeling career. I photographed her once in the summer and once in the winter. She wrote the words enclosed below in response to her summer portrait. She was both happy and unhappy with it.

Although the winter portrait was stunning, I prefer the August photo, and I hope Vivi would too. To my eye, she was more comfortably exposed.

> "Everything I see is proof of . . . the road(s) I have taken, and I am gloriously, profoundly happy to say I can see that the child still lives!"

Vivi

Not until I saw this portrait did I know that Vonnie was shoeless in the snow. Yikes!

"So I was thinking about all those cold feelings I experienced from this exercise, and when I look at the photo, it almost seems to me that I'm posing on a beach or something. Why wasn't I yelling and screaming at you to hurry up? Why doesn't my face show the pain of my cold feet?"

Vonnie

Carolyn and I thought that we were at an out-of-the-way site. After she dressed again, a snowplow came around the corner. I hope that the driver would have been unfazed if he/she had seen a naked woman, knowing that this place was Goddard College, and this state was Vermont.

"My writing . . . is working towards connecting my head with my body. When I look at this picture, I feel like I'm halfway there."

Carolyn

As Michelle and I ambled slowly to the spot she had chosen for the portrait, we talked about our problems with body image. She said, "I don't think I can do this." We stopped and I fiddled with my camera on the ground. I then slowly stood up again to find her in front of me fully naked. I am glad she felt empowered.

> "As you took my photograph, I didn't think too much about my body, or how I was standing, or how I looked. The layers were gone and it felt like I was open and connected to you through your lens. There was a confidence in that relationship. Trust . . . Through your eyes, you gave me the gift of comfort.
>
> "Thank you."

Michelle

Caryn and I ducked secretly into an upstairs room with fading window light. I evaluated the scene, the light potential, and I decided to go quickly. But before I started snapping pictures, I lowered my camera and asked her, "May I just look?" I think that both of us were uncomfortable. It could have been so easy to hide from her behind my viewfinder. And so we went on, feeling that the connection had been made.

"When Rhonda . . . asked me to pose, I told her yes, thinking it would be good for me. Besides, I wanted to contribute to putting out into the world images of bodies like mine . . .

"I looked more deeply into the camera in a way I never had before . . . I knew that however this photo came out, it would really be me. I also knew that it would hurt to look at it, that I would have to find a way to see, a new way . . .

"As I breathe in my body, I am so much more aware of how anything can happen. In that anythingness, there's so much room to get lost, and also so much to find."

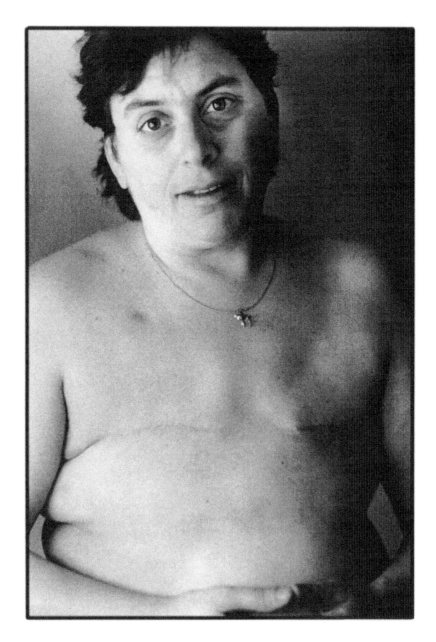

Caryn

Grandma has not written words, but I have included her because she declared to me, "I am not right for your project. I have always loved my body."

Grandma

Despite a lack of words and verbal expressions, the image of Lily is eloquent. It "speaks" simply and profoundly about innocence; about freedom.

Lily

Traumatized thinking: Split-off or isolated thinking, which is the result of disconnection of some bodily structures from the rest.

ellie epp and friends, regarding the MA in

interdisciplinary studies, writing at goddard college

For now, just look, and look again.

This, then, is to respect.

laura sewall, *sight and sensibility*

Would you let me photograph you?

After women have viewed the *Bodies in Focus* portraits, I like to ask this question. Although I cannot now photograph you, I am still interested in how you would answer.

NO: If you say no, is it because you love or respect yourself in such a way that you draw boundaries to control access to your body?

NO: If you say no, is it because you lack respect for or even hate your body, yourself?

YES: If you say yes, what would you value about the experience?

Quoted from Laura Sewall's
Sight and Sensibility

And if the incoming streams of
light, sound, and scent coalesce
with a presence of mind and a truly
participating body, perception may
become the ground for a sensuous,
even ecstatic relationship with the
world.

Darsan [Hindu concept] implies
being gifted by the thing seen in
a moment when the observer is
receptive and respectful, and thus
able to truly see.

When we allow the images and
sounds, the touch, feel, and
substance of the world to enter us,
we become the world . . .

BODY LETTERS

The following are a couple of my letters to the photographed women, the continuation of our body dialogue after the portrait sessions. Just as women's voices can be lost in silence, so too their bodies. After photographing women naked I knew that unless I was careful, silence would seep into the project. I felt desperate that their bodies not be lost, so I sent them musings here and there about the portraits—words about their bodies—hoping they would respond with similarly candid meditations. They did.

Letter One: August

Hey Beauties!

This is Rhonda, the keeper of your images. I just had the contact sheets returned yesterday. They're great for many reasons!

First off, thanks for the honor of photographing you. It was the highlight of my time—though it wore me out. I enjoyed our little "escapes" into bathrooms and trees and meditation spaces. If everyone else only knew! It helped me to overcome a pretty big hurdle regarding photography.

I will soon be printing many of the images, with view to an exhibit. I'll show them to you at the next get-together, so you can okay them for the public.

I would appreciate some little bit of writing about the experience. It can be a couple of sentences, a longer writing piece, poetry, a freewrite, etc. It's nothing to worry about.

Feel free to write if you have questions about your particular pics. By the way, I'll have my camera in February. I have visions of boots and snow and . . .

Thanks again! Rhonda

Final Letter: December

Hey Beauties!

Remember that opening from before? This will be my last group note to you all who are even more beautiful to me now that I have spent a few months with your images and words.

Thanks for your participation in what has turned out to be a very interesting and wonderful project. I have loved receiving your writing on the process and on first seeing your images. Seeing your words together is pretty revelatory.

For instance, so many of you had a breast comment that expressed a sort of surprise at seeing them reflected back to you like that. Your words together with some of my own feelings, made me wonder why we're not very aware when it comes to our own breasts.

I wanted to share with you what spending so much time with your images has done to me. It's quite a cool comment on our connection. Remember when I referred to myself as the keeper of your images? I meant then that I had your images on negatives. I can say the same thing now about being a keeper, but it means something entirely different.

I have spent so much attentive time with your images: looking at contact sheets, choosing and printing one image, having them photocopied and sent to you, hearing your words in response to them, and spontaneously flipping through all of the originals together. And what has happened as a result is that to say that I am a keeper of your images is to say that they are now stored in my body. When I think "woman," your images and what I know of you individually inform my thoughts. I needed that. Hope that's okay. Couldn't help it.

It's pretty cool. Your images have changed me. When I thanked you for the gift of your bodies, I had no idea of the extent to which they would be a gift. Whew! I hope this information isn't too bizarre. If you agree to have your image seen by others—at least by one another—I'm testifying now as to what might happen to the viewer.

Consider this note a little bit of personal exposure to make us even. I almost think it might be easier to strip, though.

I'll hopefully see you all in February.

Love, Rhonda

WILL TO PHOTOCOPY

I wake, roll to my stomach, and lift the shade to check the weather. The window is wet and cold. With my finger, I make circles in the condensation and then touch my forehead. I know what I have to do, but my body doesn't feel like doing it.

I roll over again to my back and throw the covers off my legs to cool them. The lower part of my body is really numb, and I'm so hot. I know I won't walk well this morning, but I have to go out. As I consider the ceiling, I remember when I used to wake up early to run. That was five years ago. How will I be five years from now? I'm frustrated.

I think about this book: body awareness. Is this the road to intense living, this lying here, numb and pissed-off, this remembering what I used to do, while dreaming of what I want to do?

I sit up, drop my feet to the floor, stand, and support my wobbly self with a wall. I take a step with my right leg. It feels strong, as always. But my left leg won't lift. I suspected this would happen today, a day when I need my legs. I slide my left leg across the hard wood up to the right. I move forward.

I hear Mike in the kitchen. I step . . . slide . . . step . . . slide into the very nearby living room and fall facedown onto the futon. Mike hears me and appears with a glass of ice water and a kiss on the forehead. I roll over; sit up; take the plastic, orange cup carefully in both hands; and thank him.

"Why are you up so early?" he asks.

I squint at the clock. It's nine.

"I have to photocopy," I say.

"Do you want me to do it?"

"No, this is *my* thing." My body is starting to feel stronger from the ice water. "Actually this is a woman thing."

Mike leaves for work. I enliven enough from the ice water to make green tea. I opt for a tea bag instead of loose because I need to conserve my energy for photocopying. I eat a PowerBar with my tea and take a heat sensitivity pill. Every time I stand, I feel stronger.

I think about showering. I remember back to when I took my last one, put my glasses on, walk into the bathroom to look in the mirror, and then decide to get dressed. I grab my favorite, ripped-up jeans and aim my right foot through the pant leg without getting it caught in my large kneehole. I lift my left leg with both hands and clumsily drop it through the other pant leg.

I wear two different socks. My left one goes all the way to my knee. My right hangs at my ankle. I follow my two different socks with sturdy urban hiking boots. One has a leg brace already in it which stretches as high as my left sock. After I'm dressed, I stand and feel ready to photocopy.

I open the box with all of my retouched photographs. I flip through them meditatively, like I do often, and I notice that they're dusty. I look for a small, soft piece of fabric and then brush each one off with a sock from my drawer.

I set the box on my wheelchair seat, put on my biking gloves, find my red "Flor de Caña" baseball cap, tie a sweater around my waist, and set out to photocopy. I struggle with my wheelchair out the door, off my porch, and down the grass to the sidewalk. When won't I be able to off-road like I do? When might I need a ramp?

I start pushing my chair down the sidewalk, but my left leg still won't lift. After about twenty steps, I'm so fatigued that I need to sit. I set the brakes on my chair, put the box in my nifty black wheelchair backpack, sit on the seat, take off the brakes, and I'm off and rolling.

This is fun. A tire is getting flat. I don't look at the trees as I go uphill. A crack. A pothole. I approach a slight curb. I push assertively on my wheel rims, lean back slightly, and my front tires come off the ground just enough to jump up and over it.

The breeze feels good. It lifts my shirt and touches me on the belly, like a cold hand. I notice the air more when I'm sitting.

When I arrive at the door to Copy Connection, I ease out of my chair without setting the brakes: risky. I stand a few seconds hunched over my legs to let MS tremors shake through my whole body. I put the box of prints onto the seat so my chair doesn't tip backwards. I open the door, push my chair through, and park it in my usual corner.

I see Debbie sitting at her computer. Full bodied. Beautiful.

"Hi, Rhonda!" she says.

"Hey, Deb!"

We chitchat as I set my box on the counter.

"I have a pretty complicated order," I say.

She walks over to me, and we move to a private corner by the paper cutter.

"Are these more naked pictures?" she asks, quietly, furtively.

"Yes, all of them," I say. "I need them color-copied, just like before, but I need two sets. Different sizes and paper weights."

She ducks in back of the store to bring me some paper samples to feel. I finger them and choose two surfaces.

"Can you leave them for me to do when the men go home?" she asks. I hope she's not ashamed of the images. I hope she protects them.

"Sure," I say. "I'll need them later this week. I have to mail them."

"I'll have them sooner than that," she says. "How has your health been?"

"Not great. I even had a hard time getting here today."

She looks concerned. "Then I'll drop them off at your place when I'm finished. You don't need to wheel back here."

"Thanks," I say, "but I like to get out when I can. I like to try."

I smile and point to the drawer where she put my box of portraits.

"Besides, those women help me move."

BODY LANGUAGE
Voices of the Bodies in Focus Subjects

Kate

. . . my nakedness seems completely natural and necessary.

Carol

My face, breasts and stance depict a life lived fully, from the sag of the breasts from childbirth, the facial lines and . . . I'm starting to cry . . . I just really like the woman I see in this picture— I acknowledge myself in a way I don't think I ever have before.

It was a very freeing moment for me . . . a wonderful opportunity to experience my body in a totally new way . . . [It] comes at an incredibly important time in my life when I'm trying to settle into my aging body like I've never been in my body before . . . I still feel inside my head like that child struggling to understand what being a woman means, and what I see in this photograph is someone who already knows. I have a whole different feeling about myself now . . . This photo is a gift and a testimony to myself . . .

Lynn

Weird—you know how you and I talked about body image stuff and eating disorders—well, I'm noticing how selfish I get when I am in that place. This experience with the photo and even with writing to you right now is helpful and reminds me to be grateful and loving with myself and others.

Anne

My body is present . . . [My] face doesn't seem as embodied as my body . . . I think you have captured me exceptionally well, particularly the part of me that feels strong, capable, a little hard. I have never had an image of myself that feels as real.

Jeanne

. . . I stood there, asking what to do with my hands and which way you wanted me to look and how should I stand, busying myself with the obvious physicalities, but inside, my spirit stood with arms outstretched, face turned upward, and frolicked like a wind-blown leaf on the unobstructed, freshly mowed lawn.

Debbie

On viewing this picture and seeing myself in a different way, I began to consider that I should see myself more compassionately.

Favor

In this time of abundance, odd that she should be so hungry.

Emily

I was actually cognizant enough to sleep without my underwear . . . I was like, note to self: Do not wear underwear the night before you do pictures with Rhonda as it leaves pink lines in your thigh fat.

I'm standing behind [Rhonda] while she fiddles with the key to her room . . . People walk past us. I have this sneaky feeling that nobody knows what we were just up to—like we just had sex or something. It feels that secretive and intimate to me . . . It feels like being really awake.

Carolyn M.

The first time I looked at the photos, a voice inside my head said, 'God, you're ugly.' But that is the old story . . . I went out to buy a magnifying glass to prove that [the voice] was wrong. I inspected the [contact sheets] then like a scientist or researcher looking for clues that my body had some redeeming qualities . . . [In] the photos where I am clowning around, there is a . . . joyous light quality. That light is who I really am. It's seeping out of every curve, every pore . . . I want to tell that voice inside me that is saying, 'God, you're ugly' to SHUT THE FUCK UP! I'm gorgeous.

Andi

. . . the fire I feel inside is invisible in the body.

Ana

I write different versions of what I feel, and deep down I have the feeling that nothing I've written is frank enough: They are all versions, versions of a woman's insecurity about her body. Masks. It is like, unless I make a story for this, unless I surround this image with my words, make it mine, I will not be able to deal with the fact that I am there, in the middle of a Vermont forest, knee deep in the snow, naked and grinning.

I want to thank you for the experience, Rhonda . . . for putting us at the edge with ourselves.

Vivi

Everything I see is proof of . . . the road(s) I have taken, and I am gloriously, profoundly happy to say I can see that the child still lives!

Vonnie

So I was thinking about all those cold feelings I experienced from this exercise, and when I look at the photo, it almost seems to me that I'm posing on a beach or something. Why wasn't I yelling and screaming at you to hurry up? Why doesn't my face show the pain of my cold feet?

Carolyn

My writing . . . is working towards connecting my head with my body, and when I look at this picture, I feel like I'm halfway there.

Michelle

As you took my photograph, I didn't think too much about my body, or how I was standing, or how I looked. The layers were gone and it felt like I was open and connected to you through your lens. There was a confidence in that relationship. Trust . . . Through your eyes, you gave me the gift of comfort.

Thank you.

Debby

morning shadows
tickle my nose
a smile appears
reminding me
i am free
i am beautiful

Caryn

Each day I walk among the other bodies, lately not so concerned with glancing at women's breasts, the ones not cut away and replaced by imposters. Sometimes I remember to remember that everyone has their own scars and numbness, most of these wounds are not even physical.

When Rhonda . . . asked me to pose, I told her yes, thinking it would be good for me. Besides, I wanted to contribute to putting out into the world images of bodies like mine . . .

I looked more deeply into the camera in a way I never had before . . . I knew that however this photo came out, it would really be me. I also knew that it would hurt to look at it, that I would have to find a way to see, a new way.

The shot that spoke to me the most though was one I didn't remember Rhonda taking. I was standing, my hands barely touching over my stomach. My head was tilted just a bit to one side. I looked scared, calm, happy, sad, steady, relieved. The things I didn't like about my appearance were there—the dark circles about my eyes, my lack of a firmly defined chin, the hair that has its own agenda, and the extra weight. The pockets of fat at my sides were caught in the spotlight after years of being upstaged by the star power of the breasts. I could see the faint scars across my chests, the spot where the chemo port went in and out, and the whiteness of my skin.

All my pre-adult life fast-forwarded to now. I had fretted about my body in the boring and usual way just about every other woman I've ever known has, and that old hatred and worry filled the background of each photo [on the contact sheet]. Yet in the center of each, there was just me, just a 44-year-old woman with some of her trails and trials more visible than others. It wasn't what I would call sexy or beautiful, yet it was alive. Erotic, I suppose, if I'm brave enough to claim that word.

As I breathe in my body, I am so much more aware of how anything can happen. In that anythingness, there's so much room to get lost, and also so much to find.

IV

RELEASE
The Mind of Opening, Expanding, and Letting Go . . .

___

[The erotic is] . . . those
physical, emotional, and
psychic expressions
of what is deepest and
strongest and richest
within each of us . . .

**audre lorde, "uses of the
erotic: the erotic as power"**

Seven-Minute Timed Freewrite

I walk down the lonely, cloud-covered beach and throw my clothes to the sand and spin and spin naked in circles like reality, like a prayer wheel dancing my body sacredly through natural things. I am sand and wind and ocean and I move among and with. I hear my breath like a breaking wave. I feel my breath like a Santa Ana wind, sweeping me up in its warm abandon.

I float down the river naked. I take my shirt off at 14,000 feet, and my arms are outstretched as if I will fly into a whole new world. I see my breath. I hold Mike to me and we rest here in this melting of skin. The sun kisses my breasts. I close my eyes in a rainstorm. I climb a cottonwood tree, branches scraping across my stomach and lifting my hair. Holding me. Danger here, but when I risk a fall, moving up and up, I see the world around and below. I know where I am.

When I open my body to the world, I feel air and hands and water and hot and cold and pain and ecstasy across and through me, and this is where I laugh and I cry. This is where I live, in this release of all that holds me, suffocating and fetal. When I go wrapping myself up in my own limp arms, and spit at the world, "Don't come in! I will not open for you!" I float like a carcass down the Ganges. I am bloated. I am decayed and oozing, and my eyes don't reflect faces or other sources of light.

Release is about running naked into the arms of death, embracing it like a lover, sitting with death, letting it stroke my hair, and speaking to it of what I know and of what I see and of the world I feel across my skin, and showing it how I can spin naked through the sand, even when I can't move my legs.

"Delight in non-clinging," say the Buddhists as they rest like a lotus, drinking tea. If I let go, will I fall through life like a brilliantly rolling gem? If the falling is the polishing, will I shine as I slip away?

"Opening" Introduction

I am slowly learning to release.

Releasing is a discipline that requires awareness of my maniacal gripping tendencies, while still attentively abandoning myself to movement, because my body wants to move regardless of theories and of knowing the outcome.

Releasing requires listening to my body in the moment; letting go of inhibition; freeing shame and silence through expression; being vulnerable enough to love openly; attending to sensation as it caresses my body; and letting fall away from my life anything else that might work to wrongfully obstruct my motion, whether in moving down the street or in thinking through a concept. When I release control of my body, I realize the exhilaration of purer movement.

My biggest challenge of releasing pertains to letting go of the hypercontrol I assumed over my body. In my sand dream, the sand is initially irritating as it pours from me. At first, I anxiously try to stop it, and I feel angry and hateful toward myself as I work to ignore it but can't. In not being able to release control and let the sand flow, I felt desperate and unhappy. I felt the same way when I denied that disease was changing my body, my life. I was blindly trying to hold onto something I couldn't.

As a discipline of body awareness, the writing of this book is a practice of release.

But release is not just letting go of illusory control and of old and debilitating ways of being. At the same time that I let go, I must open myself to a fuller experience of being a body in the world. When I'm bravely aware of how my body occupies space, I more easily and meditatively do the work of letting go and embracing. When I release attentively and willingly, I am not desperate.

This section contains pieces that are specific meditations on different kinds of releasing. I hope they catch me in the act.

SILENCE INTO LIGHT

---

*My work is to inhabit the silences with which I have lived and
fill them with myself until they have the sounds of brightest day
and the loudest thunder.*

audre lorde, *the cancer journals*

I'm freeing a silence.

In her book, *The Lover Within: Opening to Energy in Sexual Practice*, Julie Henderson says my identity is as an energetic body, capable of intense rushes of ecstatic energy—even as I'm grocery shopping. She warns against being ashamed of or inhibited by this identity, by my body. Release, she says. Let your body open and shame slip away.

As I read Henderson's words, a story from my past demands to be told for the first time. In speaking this silence now, I feel a strange rush of energy. Maybe the energy results from releasing the shame that had crept into the unique experience. Maybe the energy comes from acknowledging and celebrating my body's natural will to pleasure. I don't know. I just feel really good.

I lived in Santa Barbara during the spring and summer after my college graduation there. I didn't like to go to the beach with its sunny-day clutter of people and affectation, but wandered lonely when it was overcast, a little cool and windy. I would take my blanket, dress warmly, and lie peacefully on the sand—closing my eyes and curling up in the ease and sensuality of it all.

As I was lying on my stomach one day, a mysterious, foreign, and quiet man approached me and asked if he could give me a back rub. I'm careful. I intuit danger and slimeballs pretty well. Without really turning around to get a good look at him, I perceived him as oddly safe. I let him do it.

During the back rub, I was relaxed, listening to the waves and feeling the breeze. Soon, his hands felt like they were vibrating, and my whole body began pulsating. He wasn't touching me in the genital area, but I felt like I was climaxing. I was.

In a rush of wind and ocean and body, I had an orgasm. Silently, the man left. I lay there for a while after, feeling it. I was euphoric. The world and how I felt it was different. The "rules" of my body had changed. Intense energy raced through me. I remember it still.

It's not that I had never experienced orgasm before. Though when it happened, I had still never had intercourse—had never even kissed anybody. For years I was told that sex was sinful, so I avoided connecting my body with another. I touched myself, though. I masturbated alone in my sin. Strange the reasoning that counts a lonely sinner as a lesser sinner and that says I should hide my pleasure.

After the back rub, I must have been glowing as I went around in a joyful stupor, feeling my new experience as a body. I remember avoiding acquaintances the whole day in order to wander through town, down to the wharf, and around the cliffs. I drank coffee alone on Lower State Street, perused bookstores alone on Upper State Street, and ate lunch alone on the pier.

As I consider the time now, I wonder if I avoided other people in order to be with my new, *pure* experience as a body. Was I avoiding negative judgment as I did after I accidentally discovered orgasm in my shower? The bathing pleasure was also intense, new, and *pure*. However, the purity of it was lost to other people's labeling. In a sense, I lost my body then.

Did I know that as soon as I returned to my Santa Barbara community, even if I didn't tell others about the beach surprise, I would have my memory of the experience suffocated by an understood group value? The experience would be labeled "bad." I would be labeled "bad." Did I want to be left alone for a while to enjoy *pure* pleasure?

After that day, I began to abstract the experience by analyzing it. Was it a sexual encounter? Was I still a virgin? Was I asking for something by letting a strange man "have his way" with me on the beach? Was it just a back rub and nothing more? Did he have any idea of what he was doing and of what happened to me? Okay, so maybe I was naïve.

Because I was so dizzied by my will to define it, and because it really didn't fit into any category I knew of, I decided to just forget it had happened. I never told a soul and tried not to think about it. Whenever I did, I felt somewhat ashamed. For over a decade, I never recovered the *pure*, ecstatic feeling of that *pure*, ecstatic time with the ocean and the wind and the sand and the man.

I never recovered the purity of the experience until writing this piece. Julie Henderson's words gave me the will to explore my identity as energy through my attentive release of shame. I think also of bell hooks' entreaty to free voice. The freeing of a voice of the past, she says, is really the liberating of a person for a richer present. By writing this story, I incorporate a memory into my life, rather than suppress it. Consequently, I feel relieved. My body feels lighter.

Who was this man who appeared, then disappeared, like a *body prophet* ushering in a new dispensation for me? Now I remember the time openly, humorously, and fondly—and not as an inherently dirty occasion. The incident was not at all about virginity or sexual promiscuity. Such concepts blur its reality, I believe. Was it simply and beautifully about my body's identity as energy and how it leapt so naturally toward pleasure? That's the meaning I attribute it from this perspective, anyway.

A Spanish way of saying "give birth" is "*dar a luz*," which literally means "give to light." Because I have brought a hidden story out of my body *into the light,* my experience as a body is given life.

DANCING

I used to leave before the dance started. I liked to join friends in sitting to watch the dancers, but the thought of so many exuberantly moving people intimidated me—and reminded me of before.

The production ends. I don't leave. Reflexively and nonchalantly I jab my fist into my gut to see how my bladder is doing. It feels okay, so I beeline toward the alcohol.

I fill the bottom of a Styrofoam cup with straight vodka. I think about first having another beer, but the alcohol content seems inadequate at a time like this—a time when people are already beginning to move rhythmically around me. I feel dizzy, see a semi-removed place on the wooden bleachers, grab yet another cookie on the way to it, and I lean there, cup and cookie to my mouth, knees pulled way up across my chest and face. I'm wearing my winter hat and coat in case I leave. I like the dim lights.

From my distance, I observe the buzz of the room, from milling margin folk to those falling onto the dance floor and abandoning their bodies to the music. If I let my eyes' focus go limp, which the alcohol helps, I just see one big blob of movement, like an amoeba. The center seems to be shaking ecstatically, while the corners gently sway. I lift my cup to my lips and vodka spills all over the front of me. My body jerks. I laugh.

I straighten my knees to the floor and take my wool hat off. I let my eyes slip in and out of amoeba-mode, but from either perspective the movement is stunning. I feel jealous, then nostalgic, then proud of the movers, then . . . then . . . then . . . I think I might cry. I set my vodka down.

Friends sometimes fall from the dance floor to sit a while with me, and although we try to scream small talk over the music, I'm more mesmerized by our rhythm of nodding our heads and smiling. I feel cozy, like the room is holding me. I take off my down vest. Scott must see me feeling my body because he grabs my hands.

"Wanna dance?" he asks. "I'll hold you."

I don't hesitate, and I literally fall with him onto the dance floor. I grip both of his hands tightly and test my legs. They won't move much, but they're not giving out. I attend to my upper body to feel the rhythm sway it from side to side. I fly my arms in the air with his. I'm leading.

As I get braver, he holds just one hand and we attempt some shaky spins. I'm dizzy and laughing, then I run into somebody. It's Ana. I photographed her earlier in the week: a Colombian woman fully naked in a snowfield.

Ana startles, recognizes me, grabs my free hand, and I have twice the support, which lets my legs collapse and recover, collapse and recover. I throw myself forward, and they catch me and pull me upright. I fall backward, and they have learned our rhythm. I'm not scared about my improvisation.

When the song ends, I can hardly stand, but I hug Scott. He's still holding me and helps me to walk back to my spot on the bleachers, where I collapse in a little puddle of vodka. My legs and arms are tingly, and I'm breathing hard. I look back to the dance floor, smiling, seeing beautiful movement. I don't let my eyes go limp again.

INCONTINENCE

One night in a Nicaraguan bar, over Nicaraguan beer, Erinn told of how the Magee women loved to lose control. Her grandma, her mom, and her aunt would circle-up together to imbibe, inebriate, and "bullshit," Erinn said. Eventually their general revelry spilled over into uncontrollable laughter and spastic bladders.

"They all just sat around and peed their pants," Erinn laughed, as we both grabbed another beer. "And they thought it was hilarious! They loved the messiness!"

As my own story in *The Vagina Monologues* tradition makes its way to my friends around the world, and as they respond to me with their own writings or testimonies—sometimes funny, sometimes serious—about orgasm and masturbation, I feel we are all inebriating in a circle.

One woman says, "I have only had one orgasm in all my life" (almost fifty years). She's inebriating . . .

Carol brightens up as she lauds the "freshness" of Aveda rosemary-mint shampoo suds. She's inebriating . . .

Another friend wants a shower massager for Mother's Day. Inebriating . . .

Erinn says that masturbation doesn't work for her, but that she is "touchy feely" with her vagina. "I love how my pussy smells." Inebriating . . .

I am witnessing how vulnerability through language, intoxication by previously unspoken words, opens some kind of personal and communal floodgate. I am witnessing how what was once scary can be yelled from mountaintops and across oceans as others circle around laughing and awaiting a chance to lose control too.

ECSTASY

I began to turn my attention directly . . . to what I experienced,
what I liked, what excited me, what satisfied me—setting aside
all previous judgment, expectations and demands.

julie henderson, *the lover within*

It's my pleasure to share this essay.

Sometimes my crotch is numb.

I say "sometimes" because without pattern multiple sclerosis sends numbness ebbing and flowing throughout my body. It grips different body parts whimsically. The numbness can last a day, a month, a year, or never go away. My hands have been numb for ten years. I feel them, but with lessened sensation. How does this affect my life? I burn myself a lot, my handwriting is unfamiliar, and when I pick up a glass, I do it consciously, willing my fingers to grip hard . . . harder. Numbness is scary because . . . well . . . it reminds me that my body is slipping away from sensation, from a full interaction with life.

Sometimes my crotch is numb. Sometimes. When I lose sensation down there the skin feels deadened. Admittedly, during these times, I might reach for "it" in public, maybe because it feels funny, maybe because I kinda wanna in an irrational way make sure it's still there, maybe because I think a numb crotch is grounds for pooh-poohing social conventions. How does a numb crotch affect my life? My pleasure? It doesn't.

At a recent MS lecture a male neurologist had the answer to our vaginal numbness. "Frozen peas," he said. "Have your partner rub you with a plastic bag of frozen peas." Huh? He said that men need Viagra and women, bless their hearts, need frozen peas.

I felt a chill through me then, and not because I was turned on by freezer veggies or because I was imagining ice to the crotch. His inattentiveness to and ignorance of my sexuality appalled me. The frozen peas might be worth trying—why not—by anyone. While he spoke, I was numb in the crotch area. However, I had recently been experiencing intense, *new* realities of sexual pleasure. While the skin around my vagina is numb, my clitoris isn't.

We women with MS have only secondary sexual problems: For example, when I have sex, I set a glass of ice water nearby, so I can keep my body cool during the heat of passion. If my body warms up too much, I can't move well, and I have to tell Mike to "do it all" as I lie there limply. Times like this remind me of a scene in Salman Rushdie's *Midnight's Children,* in which a man asks his frigid wife to just "move a little" beneath him. Sometimes I struggle to move a little.

After the frozen peas chat, the neurologist at the lecture that day was still talking to us for a while about . . . something. His mouth was opening and closing and opening and closing, but all I could think about was sex—pleasure, orgasm.

I was wondering how my witness to sexual pleasure (which, I believe, is really an important witness to my diseased body's capacity for heightened awareness) could compete with *his* diploma? I'm sure that many of the women present also needed to hear about my experience of pleasure in general: of enjoying intense "argument" with a friend, of writing about incontinence, of watching a tree, of reading feminism, of swimming naked in a lake, and oh so much more. But considering the advice about frozen peas, sharing with the women my experience in the category of sexual pleasure seemed especially vital.

The neurologist might be an authority on how our bodies are coming apart, but I can tell of how they are still intact. I'd have the demeanor, I hope, of holding a friend's hand, staring her in the eye, and saying, this is what has happened to me ... Did you know ... ? After all, I'm indebted to feminist writers for sharing their bodies with me. Shouldn't I do the same?

But it didn't seem to be the time or place for me to defend the pleasure possibilities of our disease-ravaged bodies. And besides, I wasn't thinking to share my story only with MS-stricken women. A fantasy of mine is sitting in a circle with all sorts of women, laughing and telling one another our stories about pleasure.

But when is the time to talk about pleasure? Where is this circle? With examples, I'll begin here with a testimony of my *new* experience of heightened sensation, of sexual pleasure. I follow the piece with a timed freewrite. This sharing is for all women. I'm blushing, but here goes ...

I am thirty-five. My ten-year sex life with Mike has always been very pleasurable. I have orgasms when I want to. Not in intercourse, though (I can remember only one of *this* variety). Manually. Orally. I love touching skin. I love intimacy. The orgasm was sometimes an aside (a nice aside!), until recently. I am thirty-five, and I know new realities of ecstasy.

I'll define ecstasy as not just climax or orgasm, but more. I think of it as these experiences given depth or intensity. Ecstasy is a condition of so acutely sensing what is within and without my body that I perceive most everything differently. My *experience* of myself in the world is transformed. I feel as if my old boundaries are felled by my new awareness. I'll explain.

Ecstasy didn't just come upon me from nowhere. I needed to be taught something about my capacity for pleasure. Since I couldn't sit in circles with women, I happened to read two books, one after the other, which changed my attention to the world and to how I connect with it.

I first read Julie Henderson's *The Lover Within: Opening to Energy in Sexual Practice*, which was really about attention to self as an "energetic body." She gave exercise after exercise to help start cultivating attention to my body as a locus of pleasure. Her exercises charged me with energy which felt so pleasurable that I wondered if she were just teaching me creative masturbation. If masturbation is attention to sensation and pleasure, then yes, it *is* masturbation.

The second book, Laura Sewall's *Sight and Sensibility,* changed my attention to seeing: to think of it as an energetic exchange between two things, as bringing the world into my body. Wow! In learning to see, I was learning to feel my body.

When I used the two books to begin to inform and guide my experience, something amazing happened. With attention to energy and seeing, during sex I remain at a high plateau of pleasure for a long time. The sensation I feel is not just about the normal-for-me pleasure of moving toward climax. In a way, the moving is so pleasurable that occasionally I think I'm already having an orgasm—until it gets even more intense. Sometimes I have to stop what I'm doing because my pleasure is so continuous that to remain at this level for too long is unbearable. This state of acute awareness up through the full release of built-up energy is what I'm calling ecstasy. At this point, I writhe. I moan. I'm generally euphoric.

Funny! As I'm writing this, I have to constantly push myself to release the story of my experience. In letting myself go, then, I'll say a little about the pleasure *process*.

Following Julie Henderson's suggestion, during sex I begin with attentiveness to how pleasure feels in my body, by sinking my awareness into the sensation, the locus of which begins in the vaginal area. However, after I am very aware of it, feeling it and feeling it, I move this energy through my whole body. This is to say that I try to feel the pleasurable sensation as moving up my torso, through my arms, down to my feet, across my nipples. Yes, my nipples! All over! Is it too abstract to describe this as claiming pleasure as part of my body's identity? That's what I feel.

What role does seeing, does Laura Sewall's book, play in my awareness of sexual pleasure? If my eyes are open when I am in the intensely aware and pleasurable state, all

I see feels like it is rushing through my body. This is powerful! Stimulating! Erotic! Just as I no longer have boundaries to my own sensation (as I'm mindful of moving energy through me), I don't feel the same boundaries between the world and me. What I see and feel joined with is usually Mike but sometimes the wall . . . or light fixtures . . . oh god, the light fixtures! When I see these things from the state of acute awareness of my body, they're not as I used to perceive them. Maybe I can't really see them well because of my body's euphoric state. Maybe I just see them better than before. I would like to say that the primary visual stimulus is Mike, but that's not true. I *would* like to say it, though.

Unfortunately, there are all kinds of roadblocks to *becoming* pleasure. I can't attend to the sensation and feel it through my body if I am not semiconsciously releasing all inhibition and shame. I'm resistant even now as I'm writing this piece because I know I have to give an example of what this release means for me. Why be shy now? I'll never demonstrate release with silence. Here are two examples:

The release of past shame is one. Until I addressed it through writing, the beach orgasm incident I recounted earlier made me feel a degree of shame. The silenced story is now magically freed from my body. I can't be completely sure how the silence might have affected my attention to sensation, but I think that storing up a lifetime of little shames must constrict my body, my pleasure, to some unconscious degree.

A second inhibition I need to mindfully release during an attention to pleasure is guilt about what turns me on. Specifically (while still remaining comfortably vague), if I feel physical attraction to an abstract person besides Mike, I let myself feel what that attraction does to my body. It's not grounded. It's fantasy, but it does do something real. I don't tell myself not to feel. I'm just honestly attentive to the sensation. What do I like? What makes my body writhe and seem to leap with energy? How can I continue to release guilt and inhibition so that I feel my body more acutely? For example, if a surprising fantasy pops into my head while I'm having sex with Mike, I don't work to push it away. I open myself to it, which is as simple as mindfully relaxing my vagina as the fantasy enters my consciousness. Whew!

Speaking of Mike, this testimony is hardly complete without his mention. He's my partner. He's my true love. Until I almost collapse with fatigue, he's an eager advocate of the ever-ambiguous g-spot. Although "pleasure" is wonderfully overused in this essay, I'm thrilled to say that he takes my *pleasure* very personally. With Mike I'm safe to explore my pleasure. My pleasure is his pleasure, he says, and I believe him.

Although process for me is now an intense bliss, not unlike what I used to know of climax, what happens to me during a more literal peak? When I'm climaxing and know I'm climaxing, the sensation of this through my body seems interminable. Sometimes the rush won't stop until I start to break it with exhausted laughter. It usually keeps going through it, so my experience of laughter is new also. It's ecstatic. But laughter and orgasm are already related, I think.

I'm thirty-five, and I love that there's more and more to experience as a body. Whether our crotches are literally numb from disease, or our bodies are numb to the possibility of a fuller, ecstatic sensation, the answer for all women isn't frozen peas. Even though I thought I was already doing well sexually, I have experienced intensely that pleasure isn't just an end. When it comes to my body, pleasure is also the process.

For women, ill or not, one very primary impediment to pleasure is that we're slow to tell one another our honest experiences. I'm trying.

Ecstasy Freewrite

I did this five-minute freewrite several months before I wrote the "Ecstasy" piece. I love knowing that being in touch with my pleasure began long before Sewall and Henderson. My pleasure heightens as I feel my body more thoroughly and more intensely. Ecstasy is not about one linear "big bang." Process. Love that!

My body is different now that all I see, feel, hear, and touch reaches through me, and I just want to lie back and be pleasured by what surrounds me, relaxing enough to let life make love to me, stroke my skin, oh and stroke my skin and move deeper into the place where I am born again and again, oh and again, as I writhe at the love I never knew, oh and never knew, but that surrounded me and stalked me all my life, but I never knew. A little girl in the icy river, and I didn't feel a thing. A young woman looking at myself in the mirror, but cringing and shy and hateful toward a reflection that gives me joy now, so much joy that sometimes my vagina burns, and I have to go make love to myself to complete the work the senses began, saying yes yes yes, oh and yes. I live and feel and it's so good. Living, feeling, loving. Make love to the world. Let the world make love to me. I see and cry. Life is so good. Swelling of joy swelling of breasts swelling of ecstasy.

PLEASURE
Pleasure is a sensation. It is written into our bodies; it is our
experience of delight, of joy. . . . [It comes] from deep
within our bodies, tapping the wellsprings of desire and curiosity,
a knowing that resides within ourselves.
carol gilligan, *the birth of pleasure*

FALLING

The erotic is not a question only of what we do; it is a question of
how acutely and fully we can feel in the doing.

audre lorde, "uses of the erotic: the erotic as power"

I'm surrounded by falling, by people who fall. I fall too. In considering falls now, I'm convinced that my own well-being depends on my attentiveness to how bodies slip away.

A fall seems to be a socially disruptive occurrence. It is an everyday phenomenon, but as a culture we have pushed it so out and away from consciousness that a loss of bodily control stuns us wide-eyed and breathless. To be attentive to falls is overcoming a sort of numbness. Acknowledging them is a radical attention to a body as it moves and doesn't move among other bodies that move and don't move. How can we really know our bodies when we don't know falls?

Despite my own falls, I'm guilty of turning away from them in important ways. In this essay, I look at a few different falls that surrounded me within a couple of days. This discussion is my own little way of blinking and breathing through falling.

My Fall

I stepped carefully from the taxi. My legs, my body, were feeling stable, but I can never count on them to stay that way, especially with the sidewalk like it was at the airport. I held onto the shuttle door and glided the sole of my foot over the pavement. I need to know the nature of the surface I hope to pass over. I'm aware of where my feet step these days. It was icy, but I knew I would move better for knowing this.

Earlier that day, only just before the taxi ride, my body stopped altogether from multiple sclerosis fatigue. I couldn't pack my suitcase without my legs collapsing me into a pile. This is usual. I used to cry with frustration at the lack of control. I'd think of death, too. I don't anymore. I just rest and try to cool myself. I feel my body better when it's cool. A chill helps nerve conduction. That's scientific—and my body says so.

A glass of ice water is my usual coolant, but since I would be flying later that day with my impetuous bladder, I planned to avoid liquids. And so, as my body doubled when I was packing, I struggled to a porch and sat outside in the cold, snowy morning until I felt it again. Knees to my face. Cheeks in my hands. I could see my breath. Henry wondered if I were meditating.

Back to my fall: I stepped carefully from the taxi. My legs, my body, were feeling stable. My suitcase was lowered from the trunk to my side. I eyed it and test-lifted it off the ground. So heavy, just like my carry-on, but I overstuff like I do so I can carry fewer bags when I travel alone. People will help. I feel pride, though, in doing the simple movements when I can, while I can.

I piled my backpack on my suitcase with wheels. I should be just fine, I thought. I aimed myself toward the airport door and stepped forward.

I fell.

I can't say much about the falling—the exactly why, the exactly how. Falling is such an unconscious occurrence that I don't consider mine more fully until after.

I do remember when I initially became more conscious, when I realized I was sprawled face- and belly-down across the sidewalk with busyness around me. A woman—don't know who—presented the cane I had thrown across the sidewalk. Another—don't know who—righted my bags. Other faceless movers helped me to my feet.

They were faceless because I in my fallen state had ceased to see and feel. Or rather, I was so damned embarrassed that I was pretty much in a fog. I didn't feel my body because I was rushing to stand and pretend that nothing much had really happened. I wasn't aware of my emotions because, again, I was too busy with the work of cover-up, of pretending that I was normal and that a face-plant of that caliber was everyday. I even insisted on trying again to tote *my own* luggage until Phil ignored me and rolled off with my suitcase.

When others see me crash, they do stop, they do look, but they feel uncomfortable and maybe helpless. I see the desperation in their eyes. They see me, but fearfully, not mindfully. Maybe they second-guess their response, fear that they will treat me insensitively. Maybe my fall makes them fear their own mortality. Maybe they really fear that I might be hurt. Despite the exact provocation of the feeling, acute vision and fear can't coexist. Fear erases.

How do I see myself fall, *feel* myself fall? Do I erase myself? Am I numb? I ask because with such a strong will to cover-up, I don't think I really know my own falls. I fall with embarrassment, with shame. Do I affect a false strength? These are real feelings to be acknowledged, but there is more to feel. I knew there had to be more.

Can I fall with attention to how I crash? Feel my body crumpled? Know my body crumpled? Be fully aware of my myriad feelings afterward? Can I be mindful even when others aren't? I'm trying . . .

Dani's Fall

I saw her fall twice in one day. I never witnessed the actual slip. I only saw her on the ground. Seeing her there where she didn't go willingly, I was attentive and moved. Is it because I care about her or because I fall myself? I don't think I can separate the two.

I saw Dani fall: her legs doubled beneath her; her body so close to the ground; the snow on her left pant leg; water marks; blouse contorted, lopsided; straightening her shirt, her back, her shoulders; standing and brushing; holding onto a slide carousel, to a drink; saving the rest; a pained look turned . . . distant?

I felt Dani fall, which is about my own feelings when I saw her on the ground. I felt fear for her body, for her slides. I felt frustration at our distance, that I couldn't reach out like I wanted to, needed to. I felt pride for how she moved. I felt empathy, felt the feelings of my own falls, the emotions that come from disrupting what seems smooth. When she fell, many people in the vicinity stopped moving. We seemed to be holding our breath. Sometimes, as a culture, we are unfamiliar with falls because the physically challenged person doesn't move her body in such a way as to risk falling. This isn't as much about a fear of physical injury (though the risk is real) as about a fear of cultural eyes.

I am reminded here of the many physically disabled women in my town who don't leave their homes. She, the challenged mover, limits her movement, fearing that others would see her real situation. Her own bodily state embarrasses her into hiding. We just don't see her because she's not there to be seen.

I saw and felt Dani fall. Does she know that? She probably had no idea that my eyes were on her, that I was seeing as somebody raised in this fear-of-falling society, as somebody who has been there on the ground, and as somebody who cared about her body. I saw her well.

I learned from Dani's falls, too. They affected my attention to my own. Before disease, I always moved with risk of falling. If I hadn't risked, I wouldn't have lived. And now that my bodily capabilities are altered, I sometimes don't know how to move. Dani risks and models risk. I would be lying if I denied that she's a model partly because of her physical challenges. However, more truthfully, she's just a generally wonderful mover, and that's important for me to witness.

I fall well because I saw Dani fall. Will others fall well because they see me fall? Can I be acutely attentive to my own falls? My well-being, acceptance of my whole body, depends on a brave awareness of my movement.

Lise's Fall

Lise isn't physically disabled, but she fell. It's important for me to consider her fall because it was the fall of a healthy person. To fall when supposedly healthy (and I think of my initial diagnosis of MS here) is a different kind of shock to the faller and to the viewer. It's completely unexpected.

I didn't witness Lise's cross-country skiing accident, but I saw her right after. I saw more than her bandaged nose. I saw her, imagined her experience, and felt empathetically. What I saw in Lise: She was shaken up, and she hadn't fully considered the fall yet—as I was then considering it. It made her bleed. The wound was proof of pain and proof that her body had recently broken. That's traumatic.

Might she have felt a shock from this complete bodily surprise? Might she have felt pain, but somehow removed herself mentally from her body? Might she have ignored her body as a nuisance, as something that got in the way of her aims, her plans? Yes, maybe I'm projecting here.

Lise kept going, kept skiing afterward, she said—which is important to note. Our lives are usually too busy for falls. My life was much too busy for my MS fall. Lise's fall is about my fall. And my fall is about her fall. Might she understand me better as she fully considers her own? Am I understanding myself as I consider hers?

Kendra's Fall

Kendra had a seizure. Her health has been poor for quite a while. She doesn't walk well, so a fall would not be so surprising if she weren't *completely* knocked out by it. I don't know if she lost consciousness before or after she hit the ground. Either way, she was unconscious there on the floor, and that was startling. It's just not the place to be, I thought.

Hers was a new degree of falling for me to witness. Although nobody is fully conscious of a fall, of the instant, Kendra was unconscious for some time. This reality brings up an important question for me: Do I hold to a falling hierarchy based on control? To what extent does culture? As I stood helplessly over Kendra, I was concerned, of course, but also maybe relieved that I didn't fall like she did. Just maybe—if I'm honest.

If I felt that way about Kendra's fall, other able-bodied people must view my falls with a degree of thankfulness that they don't lose control like I do. Do I need Kendra's disability to feel better about my own body? Do others need my ailing body to feel more "alive"? In other words, does the existence of physically disabled people in culture promote dissociation from one's own falls, from one's own feelings, and, therefore, from one's own body?

Although every fall is personal and cannot be cleanly categorized, I have just discussed what I consider to be three types of falls. That Dani and I lose occasional control is not too much of a surprise to anybody—to us or to witnesses. Lise's crash was a surprise to all of us, but pigeonholed as unfortunate and isolated. Kendra's was scary to me, as it represented a total loss of bodily control.

Despite my own falls, I see how I still dissociate from the full experience. I think that true and intense aliveness depends on a brave and honest attention to falls—to mine and to others. In other words, to live fully as a body, I need to pay attention to how it slips away.

I imagine that a fall disrupts the smooth day-to-day bustle of life, much the way a stone pitched onto a glassy lake creates poignant ripples. But I find such tranquility in the ripples, spreading and circling, and on and on. They catch my eye. I don't look out to where the lake might be undisturbed. I focus on where the surface was broken, and I find such beauty there.

Can I open and expand through life like a ripple? Breaking. Feeling how I move rhythmically? There is such beauty here. Can I believe that?

V

ILLNESS
Mindfully Unraveling

[Well-being is] faithfully falling in love with the poignancy of being alive.

**joan iten southerland,
"body of radiant knots"**

When I was first diagnosed with multiple sclerosis, friends and family assured me that my identity was still intact, that my true self wasn't about my body anyway.

"You're still you," they would say.

"Your soul is all that really counts," some would "comfort."

I believed them initially, since their words confirmed a "truth" I had always been taught by language, philosophy, and cultural images: that my physique is subordinate in worth to my mind, spirit, soul, and all the rest of those intangible, abstract, and invisible more real aspects of my identity. I could remain comfortably numb to the new conditions that disease brought to my life, until multiple sclerosis symptoms started affecting every corner of my being.

As MS changed my life socially, physically, and even intellectually, I felt initial guilt that I couldn't detach from the temporal conditions of my body to live in the "reality" of "pure spirit." After much emotional agony, I realized that if I hoped to live well— live at all—I needed to be mindful of disease. MS compelled me to reject easy answers and to painfully consider my identity as a body.

The sand dream that opens this book is revelatory. In it I crash to the ground despite obsessively trying to protect my body; I realize that although I don't have a surface scratch from my fall, I'm really hurting inside; I'm horribly irritated by the sand that is pouring from me; and, finally, I sit meditatively and watch the sand as it makes a pile. If the sand represents MS—the decomposition or the loss of energy that results from the disease—my dream suggests that well-being depends on sinking my attention into my ill body as it slips away.

To meditate on my disappearing self is to be mindful of the daily reality of my sometimes-painful lameness, of incontinence, of numb feet and hands, of visual impairment, of fatigue, and of how I can and can't move. Only in looking bravely and mindfully at my limitations, do I live psychologically present enough in my life to have genuine vision for what I can do as a body and true passion behind every movement. I'm living more intensely, I think, because I'm mindfully aware of how I'm dying.

In this section I write about details of multiple sclerosis, about a past emotional low due to illness, about how my body connects with other bodies of my present, about a fearful experience with MS treatment, about a socially taboo release of control, and about how I still move meditatively through the present.

After I compiled pieces into this section on illness, I can more confidently assert that I am my body anyway.

DESPERATELY ILL

I am desperately ill. I think I can say it, and I need to say it. "Desperate" in the sense that my illness is serious: chronic, progressive, a relentless unraveling, a never-ending attack on my body by my body. It began for me at age 28, the average age of diagnosis for women and especially devastating for its disruption of vocational prime.

I don't even want to talk about it. I'm frightened. Dying soon isn't likely, even though so many people tell me they *knew* somebody with multiple sclerosis. Past tense: *knew.* But even if I don't die until I'm eighty, I don't want to miss out on living, on moving. I am fearfully resisting the writing of this piece. But I am desperately ill. I need to say it.

Anarchy rages through my body. I'm not alone in this general state: there's cancer, lupus, depression, and more. But I have my own special sort of anarchy.

"Your white blood cells are really confused," said my neurologist one day—slowly enough to be offensive.

Padded and imprecise words aside, the reality is that my own, my very own white blood cells (there to defend against bodily invasion) are messing with my nerves. They're eating away at the plump and fatty sheath that protects them: myelin, it's called. This condition is known as multiple sclerosis (MS). Multiple hardenings. Lots of lesions, scars, all over: on my spinal cord; in my brain; along any neurological pathway. All over.

Clinically speaking, it's a degenerative neuromuscular disease.

The result of all this "confused" preying is neurological mayhem. Nerve impulses that once raced throughout my body, abandoned like naked children, like brilliant flashes of physiological coordination, don't enjoy this sort of freedom like before. They stop at the scarred area, then either tiptoe through these roadblocks, take alternate routes, or give up conduction altogether. Consequently, I limp mostly, wet my pants if I'm not careful, and sit inert periodically.

My worst symptom and greatest challenge is fatigue. I get fatigued if I move my limbs too much, or if I get too warm, or if I have any sort of infection (even from a toe blister), or just because my disease randomly wipes me out for the day. Fatigue is almost impossible to describe to anybody who doesn't experience it. In fact, I am guilty of thinking people are really insensitive when I comment, "I'm really fatigued today," and they respond, "I know what you mean. I'm tired too."

Tired! Tired? I'd love my fatigue to be no more than the feeling after a really exhausting day. When I'm fatigued I feel as if I'm carrying 200 pounds up a muddy hill. When I'm walking fine one minute, fatigue will sometimes out-of-nowhere strike me to my knees and challenge me first to stand and then to keep going. Fatigue makes me consider every step I take because sometimes I feel that to lift a leg and move it ahead must be the greatest feat of my life. To move when I am fatigued is to move with attention, creativity, bravery, insistence, humility, and a sense of humor.

The most painful symptom I have is spasticity. Spasticity is a condition in which nerves that control muscles go firing involuntarily without a normal rhythm of stimulating some muscles to contract and others to relax. When nerves stimulate a whole group of relaxing and contracting muscles at the same time, the chaotic firing causes spasms and stiffness. Occasionally when I'm sitting, one leg might straighten and stiffen with a spasm, and I have to pause to let the spasticity pass before I can bend it again. And often when I stand from a sitting position, spastic tremors shake my entire body for a few seconds. Ironically, because the muscles of people with multiple sclerosis fire so randomly and regularly, we tend to have fairly good muscle tone. Is this a luxury?

Another symptom worth discussing is the scariest for me to even broach. MS regularly affects cognitive abilities.

"It's not like you get any dumber," said a neuropsychologist. "It doesn't affect your critical thinking."

The cognitive problem is a memory issue, and I definitely feel the symptom, especially as I'm writing a sentence and can't for the life of me remember where I was going in the first place, and how I brilliantly planned to end it. Fortunately, the memory problem is assuaged by immediately writing down every important thought. I am comforted that I'm not getting dumber, but the cognitive symptom, only recently acknowledged in the MS world, still scares me to death.

Even though my myelin can be destroyed to the point of literally bringing me to my knees, it can also regenerate. The possibility and reality of regeneration means that MS is unpredictable. As a result, many symptoms appear only sometimes. Sometimes I'm numb, sometimes not. Sometimes my left leg doesn't move, but usually it does. I have no control. I just don't know. And so fear and hope co-exist—embrace even—as they spin through my days. I have to believe that this is a creation dance with its necessary movement from occasional despair to quiet and steadfast hope.

After eating their fill of juicy protective coverings, my white blood cells are often not satisfied with only the little bit of carnage. If they were to leave the nerve alone, myelin would regenerate adeptly. But occasionally the cells ravage my nerves themselves. Imagine! And, as most researchers believe, nerves don't self-repair. Once damaged, nerves are *always* damaged. I *always* have blind spots in my eyes. My hands will *always* be numb. And might I *always* limp and lurch? Perhaps. Nerve damage shows up on MRIs as black holes in neurological tissue.

"Don't you want to know where your black holes are?" asked Kathy.

"Why would I want to know *that*?" I replied. "They can't do anything about it."

"No, but then you'd know why you can't do things," she said.

But I *can* do things. Lots of things.

Sometimes I concentrate too much on what I can't do the way I did before. I can't wander meditatively and photograph what I happen across. I can't throw nieces and nephews around in circles. However, MS probably won't alter my longevity. I'll just have difficult physical challenges throughout my lifetime. I might even be totally immobile. That's terrifying.

Though I'm only seven years into the disease progression, I'm already faced with one challenge after another. I sometimes hate that I can't make the tough decisions without MS being such a factor. For example, will Mike and I have children? We ask ourselves this question not considering how our careers will suffer. We ask this of ourselves when I struggle to walk across the room, when I am illegal to drive, and when I have to have a nurse come to my home periodically to give me IV steroids.

I used to plan and dream about how my life would be in the future. I was good at ignoring my body in the present for the sake of how I wanted it to be later. However, since my health now changes throughout the day and week, I am forced to consider my body at almost every moment. Living with such immediacy is sometimes frustrating, oftentimes scary, but always a creative adventure if I keep that perspective before me.

Since hypercontrolled stability is really a fantasy, I am doing what I love to do while I can. The alternative is not doing anything that makes me passionate because I worry about a day I might not be able to move like I am now. I'll finish this piece with a list of some of my considerations as a desperately ill, but uniquely living body:

List

- My hands are really weak today. How will I hold this book to read?
- My legs have gone inert in the pool. How will I get back to the locker room to change?

- I can't stand for too long. How will I design a sit-down darkroom?
- My body stops when it wants to. How can I still plan and carry out a photography project?
- I can't dance like before. How can I still rhythmically move my body?
- How can I prop myself in this corner and hold onto a pipe, so that I can enjoy this standing-room-only concert?
- This book's print is too light for me to see. How can I access it?
- I'm at a posh, outdoor restaurant, and my body is much too warm. Where's the bathroom, so I can wet my head?
- How fast can I go in my wheelchair, and can I take this corner in it without tipping over?
- What dreams about my future are realistic?
- I am dying and I know it. How can I live and know it?
- There's a long line for the bathroom. Where's the alley?
- How can I still be assertive with my whole body?
- They say I can't tour the Frank Lloyd Wright home with a wheelchair. Is that true? How can I do it if I want to? Who do I need to talk to about it being accessible to me?
- If I really have only so many steps in one day, how will I use them?
- How do I get to the post office when Mike is out of town?
- How do I get to a job in Des Moines when I can't drive and Mike can't take me?
- When I am visually impaired and lame, what is vision and movement for me?
- How does it feel if I stand naked in a snowstorm or if I close my eyes when I'm swimming across a lake?
- How does my skin feel as it touches Mike's? Which of us is warmer?
- If I really look closely at that light that goes bouncing from surface to surface before falling softly across your face, might my body change?
- What would it be like to live with multiple sclerosis in a developing country?

- Even though I'm visually impaired, how can I use photography to help women to feel their bodies more intently?
- My skin is numb. What does it mean to feel my entire body as it disappears?
- How will I move?

DISABILITY

As a culture, we are at once obsessed with and intensely conflicted about the disabled body. We fear, deify, disavow, avoid, abstract, revere, conceal, and reconstruct disability—perhaps because it is one of the most universal, fundamental of human experiences.

rosemarie garland-thomson, "the politics of staring: visual rhetorics of disability in popular photography"

Playing With Light

My greatest joy was light. Recording it on film was secondary, a means for imaging my love and passion. Photographs were only sparks made concrete enough to remind me later, remind me of where I came from.

Light was my vocation, my subject. With a camera and with bare eyes I studied it. I knew light. I knew it by its source and especially by what it revealed. Was it bouncing from surface to surface? Shooting in all directions through clouds, or glass, or leaves? Rays in straight lines? Wrapping around? Cradling?

Therefore, I felt profound despair at that point when I collided with early MS, with limit, losing my eyesight.

"When I consider how my light is spent," said Milton.

When I consider how my light is spent, I thought, there in my dark, my haze, there when I was motionless on the couch.

Sunny day outside then, falling through the surround windows onto my limp body, now prostrate, now supine, now fetal. Limp. Any other time before that time—all life came before that time, I thought—I would have rested there, dancing my hand in the diffused light, turning it back and forth and back and forth. Shadows and highlights everywhere. Rays flying through the room and falling all over me. I would have felt loved and alive—any earlier time.

Too much direct sun, too much contrast there on that crate, I would have noticed before that day. And that leaf is best backlit, I would have thought, since things are truer when translucent enough for light to fall through.

Another day, another time, I would be considering the light in all its joyous complexity. But not then. That day I was wondering if suicide might not be best, considering how my light was spent.

"When I consider how my light is spent," said the blind poet.

"When I consider how my light is spent," I cried, the blind photographer, thinking only of death. No light through my hands anymore.

Suicide. I had never entertained the thought before. I always had options, dreams, and a future.

Suicide. No eyes, no photography.

Suicide. No highlights, only shadows.

Thirty years old and no career.

Impossible. So I lay fetal, limp.

"Most likely to succeed," they said.

Impossible.

"A gifted photographer," they agreed.

Impossible.

"An amazing sense of light!" one exclaimed.

Impossible! Impossible!

Thirty years of hopes, dreams, and expectation culminating in my blind figure, so young and so limp. Nothing to move me anymore. Nowhere to go when there was no seeing ahead.

"Ms. Patzia," said my neuro-ophthalmologist a few days before that day on the couch, "you have the worst case of optic neuritis I've ever seen from multiple sclerosis. If your sight doesn't return in a year, it probably never will."

Never.

Suicide.

I had one more client then, soon before that day on the couch, one more subject like I loved, but to me she had no face—no eyes! She didn't know I couldn't see her like she deserved. I framed her form, used autofocus, Mike nudged me when to take the picture, and then I quit. Thirty years old and no career! No light to move by.

If no future, then why not death?

In my mid-20s, I had worked in a group home for troubled teenagers. There on the couch, I understood the group home kids' disbelief in the future and fearlessness of death. They taught us, the young counselors with life and possibility always before us, how to talk future to the kids, halfway-out-of-juvenile-hall kids, never-out-of-gangs kids, never seeing past their youth, never seeing ahead. Our words would be their eyes.

"*Tonight* a movie." "*Tomorrow* to Santa Cruz." "*Next week* the picnic." "*Next month* the roller coaster at Great America." "*Next year* ninth grade."

There on the couch, I understood them. If no future, then why not death?

Hopkins through my head then: "Not, I'll not, carrion comfort, Despair, not feast on thee; / Not untwist—slack they may be—these last strands of man / In me . . . "

That day on the couch, I was feasting on despair and played not with light, as I felt it flying from me, but with the last threads that connected me to life.

I'm not sure why they didn't untwist completely on that day, or on any other day after that. In fact, the threads that connect me to life are very tightly wound through my body as I write this.

Even though my eyesight didn't return for two years, did I move from the couch that day because I remembered how I had always lived intensely: much less about my eyes than about my entire body? Did I remember how I had played with light?

Did I remember a time like my time in Berlin, when I brought down my youth with a crowbar?

1989. Rainy and dark November morning. Alone and shaking with winter, with excitement. A borrowed crowbar. Like a baseball bat I lift it high behind my head, close my eyes, and swing it forward with enough power to splinter concrete shards from the Berlin Wall and to spread cleansing ripples through my body. Bringing down the old, the dividing, the given. I see my breath and swing back the crowbar again and again, until someone comes to ease it from me.

There on the couch, always limp, did I remember how I had lived intensely, how I had played with light?

Did I remember a time like the time I waited for wind?

1992. Rustic sailboat. Still, Egyptian air. We rest, we eight new traveling friends, beneath a makeshift canopy, until the heat pushes us jumping off the boat, yelling as we go, holding our breath as we feel the cool water envelop our blissful bodies, laughing as we surface, swimming and climbing into the boat, closing our eyes, and doing it again and again, until the wind comes to ease us up the Nile.

There on the couch, on that day that I wondered if I would ever move again, did I remember how I had played with light?

Did I remember the time that nature touched my breasts?

Hiking alone, I veer from the trail to a water hole sprinkled by light, dappled light, light through summer-blown Aspen leaves. I remove my shirt and bra, and the breeze gently outlines my arms, my breasts, that spot on my neck; I step from my shorts and underwear, and I stand tall like the Ponderosa pines shooting sturdily before me; sitting on a rock, I slip off my shoes, my socks. I am closer now. I step into the icy stream. I shudder. I lower myself to a sitting position. I shudder. I inhale deeply, close my eyes, and lie back, losing my breath, finding my breath, joyous to be gasping, to be held so ardently by the life that goes playing over me in this secret and revelatory place of ease, where I quake with leaves.

When I considered how my light was spent, there on the couch, fearful and fetal, unable to see with my eyes how rays through windows still cradled and loved me, did I *feel* something through me still? Deeply despairing, there with my eyes and imagination gone blurry, was I remembering how I used to know the world through my entire body? Was awareness of my body and awareness through my body my true source of light?

Had light never really left me? Was it not spent at all, but was my body only so terrifyingly modified by disease that I hadn't learned how to see by it: to think, to dream, and even to feel? No wonder I was paralyzed on the couch, sometimes crying, always limp, playing with no-movement, with death. But maybe acute paralysis was necessary for new vision and purer movement.

Yes, maybe I moved from the couch that day because I was only remembering back to former times of knowing the world through my body. But maybe I also moved for the simple and profound reason that I was still aware of my body as it moved through life, that I continued to play with light. Maybe Mike came home, hugged me, poured us a drink, and we sat together on the couch like we do, holding hands like we do, interlocking legs like we love, leaning together. I must have intensely felt and known my body there with Mike, apart from the sun revealed through my eyes.

Sunny day outside, falling through the surround windows onto our touching bodies. All life, all time, seems to beautifully and mysteriously begin, move forward, where bodies touch. Is touching as revelatory as light, or is it its truest source?

My greatest joy is light. Recording it on film is only secondary, a means for imaging what I know as an entire body.

GRANDMA

Grandma and I have the same cane and crave rest. And swimming allows both of us
to move a little. So we set off to the pool together one day, and I watch her amphibious
translation from water to land, she like a swamp monster without seaweed: heavy, delib-
erate motions, lifting and dropping her 89-year-old legs from water to concrete, and then
hunching and shuffling away to the locker room. I stare and want to scream after her:

"I'm sorry that you struggle like I do!"

I mimic her move from the pool—we have each other's eyes too—and find her
naked in the shower. She doesn't hide her nudity as it puckers and bends.

"Beauty," I think, and want to cling to her under the water, so neither of us washes
away. I hate the inhumanity of the light: damn fluorescents pelting us like acid rain!
Cadaver cold.

"Don't steal us from warm colors," I spit to myself, to no one. Then I laugh and cry
beneath the water of my own showerhead, amused and horrified at the unsettling power
of everyday things.

Does Grandma know I watch her, stare at her body with longing? I want her breasts
like empty flasks. I want her limbs with knobs. Cascading skin. Shriveled butt. Hair of
mist. Bones of chalk. Wilting back. Body like the future.

Old age seems the greatest luxury to me now.

MORTALITY

For me, the primary challenge at the core of mastectomy was the
stark look at my own mortality, hinged upon the fear of a life-
threatening cancer. This event called upon me to re-examine the quality
and texture of my entire life, its priorities and commitments, as
well as the possible alterations that might be required in the light of
that re-examination. I had already faced my own death, whether
or not I acknowledged it, and I needed now to develop that
strength which survival had given me.

audre lorde, *the cancer journals*

Chemotherapy in Spanish: Not in the Language Books

I'm burning up. The 45-minute drive home from Managua is always hot, and heat and
MS together strike me limp like this. I'm wilting. I can't hold up my head, and I'm riding
with my face in my hands. The chemotherapy might be affecting me too.

I turn to Mike, who is leaned forward, alertly looking out the front windshield as
he goes dodging and beeping through the countryside.

"I'm ready for the water," I gasp.

Mike waits for the closest thing to a road shoulder and pulls over, veering carefully from a slight, dark-brown man who is pushing an Eskimo ice cream cart, selling his tutti fruity treats to *campesinos*. The man looks at Mike inquisitively. Mike kindly waves him "No" as he comes to my side of our ancient but way cool Land Cruiser, opens the door, and helps me to limply slip from my seat to the ground.

He opens a full bottle of cold water, props me up with one hand, and pours it all over my head. My body jerks and air rushes into my lungs. I stand upright and smile.

"It's so amazing how quickly I come back," I say to him.

He looks happy. We hop back into the jeep. After a couple minutes of following an oxcart, we're moving assertively again. I close my eyes, loving how the air feels across my wet head. I'm silent and content, and have almost forgotten about the chemotherapy.

We approach the outskirts of San Marcos. When I see the string of pastel Spanish Colonial houses lining up as if to cheer us home, I always get excited. We stop along the road to buy three 20-cent pineapples from the back of a red pickup. We stop again for *pepinos y zanahorrias*, before arriving at our *colonia*. We inch past street-sweeping Doña Ana. Her smile is as gentle as her broomwork.

I feel a rush of anxiety. In a flash I turn to Mike. "Have we paid her this month?"

He smiles. "Yes. I'm pretty sure *you* did. You always do."

Once home, we greet Guillermo, who with a machete is hunched over and adeptly hacking at our grass. We all exchange nods and smiles. I giggle. Mike helps me inside our tiny house and then walks back to the college.

No matter where I stand in the house, all the open windows and doors fly a breeze across my body. I take off my shoes so I can feel the cool tile through my feet. I hear people and TVs in the streets. Trash is burning. With a glass of cold water from the fridge, I sit in a rustic, Nicaraguan rocking chair. The caning on the seat lets my butt breathe.

Looking from my living room out the front door, I move back and forth meditatively. I remember . . .

I'm lying on my side with a tube running into my wrist.

I can't breathe. My heart is racing.

Doctor Cisneros approaches.

"How—odd—chew?" He's grinning, oh so proud of his less-than-shitty English, but I'm not equally nice and grinny inside or out.

I'm scared.

His presence reminds me that his English is nowhere near his reputed "perfecto," which was supposed to ease my nervousness of making chemotherapy arrangements over the phone in Nicaragua. This wasn't what my Spanish books taught me: this vocab. for a scenario of poisoning myself in a foreign language. And this is not what Mom taught me either: this . . . this . . .

My body begins shaking uncontrollably.

"¿Ay, señora, está bien?" the nurse asks me, concerned. I don't acknowledge her. She covers me with a blanket.

I still shake, but I don't speak to her, until the IV starts hurting me.

"Esto me quema," I wince.

"Así es," she answers, as if my occupation of this hospital bed with this body necessitates pain.

I'm frightened. It's blue! The liquid going into my veins is blue. When the nurse first opens the chemotherapy packet, she exclaims, "¡Bien azul!"

I hear a rattle at my front gate. It's Erinn, who has only a couple of minutes to visit. I unlock the gate, she gives me a hug, says she loves me, brings love from others who couldn't get away, agrees that it's sometimes "a pain in the ass" not to have a phone, says that if I feel okay everybody plans to meet at our place tonight, repeats her promise to shave her head in solidarity if I lose my hair, and I watch after her as she bops swiftly back down the cobblestone street.

I hear another rattle at the gate. It's Juan Diego and Susana. They greet me with a cheek kiss, come in for a while, rock a while, drink some dazzlingly magenta *pithaya* juice, and ask me questions about our last photography class. We plan for Juan Diego to cook his native Brazilian food for us Thursday night, we cheek kiss goodbye, and then they head back to school.

I feel happy. I sit down again, rocking and remembering . . .

For all of the forty minutes, I'm shaking. For most of the forty minutes, I'm looking up at the disappearing blue liquid. I wonder if it's worth it: this poisoning. This poisoning of myself for the "good" of my MS-ravaged body. For only a few of the forty minutes do I avert my eyes from the blue.

I see breasts.

The room is full of images of women frolicking in water—far too silly and over-the-top breasty, all of them.

In the corner by the skeleton . . . breasts. A large, marble statue of . . . breasts. A woman leans back as if in a waterfall and thrusts out her billowy chest. I must have smiled. In my two years in Nicaragua, I have never seen that woman.

My wrist is burning.

On one wall below a photograph of Archbishop Obando Bravo . . . breasts. A painting of . . . breasts. Three women skinny-dip and wash laundry on rocks beneath mango trees. Karla never washes our clothes topless—although we have the mango tree.

I'm shaking.

On a different wall, under a diploma . . . breasts. Another painting of . . . breasts. Two totally nude and rain-soaked women with cartoon-like inflated and perky chests carry baskets of vegetables on their heads.

I look back to the blue liquid going into my vein and don't look away again.

I'm ready for the water.

I shut and lock the front door and check to see if the water is running today.

No water, but the large plastic buckets are full as usual. With both arms, I pick up the lightest one—the purple one—by its handle and heave it splashing the short distance to the back porch, where Karla has left our socks soaking in the *pileta*.

Our clothes are spread meticulously across the line, which covers the whole yard. They seem to be spraying our high, white walls with most all the colors of Nicaragua. The chaotic, green grass looks soft and feathery in this early evening light. I reach down and touch it with my toes. I can smell the orange tree.

I set my bucket of water on the cement porch and take off my clothes. I feel the air and sun across my face and shoulders. I sit on the porch with my feet in the grass and light in my face, scoop an old, large yogurt container full of the cold water, hold my breath, close my eyes, and pour it over my head.

My body jerks and air rushes into my lungs.

PARALYSIS DREAM

Dream

As I go to bed my body is so fatigued that I can hardly move. I turn to Mike next to me and ask him to set his alarm for three a.m., in order to wake me and shoot me.

"Shoot me in the head," I say, "so I'm paralyzed, but not dead."

With gun in hand, he wakes me at three. I tell him not to shoot, saying that I prefer to feel my body in pain, rather than not to feel it at all. We go back to sleep.

Dream Meditation

As I went to bed the night of the dream, my body had stopped: so fatigued that I could hardly move. My worst health in a long time. I wasn't frightened or frustrated, though. Without any hint of desperation, I was feeling my body intensely even when it didn't work. This attention is becoming usual for me.

How wonderful that despite the pain I felt in my dream, I still decided that living meant feeling my body. I chose pain over paralysis. I hope this will always be my choice as disease progresses.

SEXY

Because fear of suffering and of losing bodily control are so deeply
embedded in our culture . . . the disabled usually are debarred from
communicating their experience effectively.

anita silvers, "disability"

A Little Release

It was eerie. The incident reminded me of that battle scene in *War and Peace,* when the
protagonist is wounded in the war zone but benignly enough to lie supine in the midst
of gunfire and death, meditatively considering the play of light and clouds. He was
removed, comfortably numb, even in the middle of the greatest apocalypse.

That's how I felt as I lumbered home from a midday swim at the community pool,
stopped in the grass along the fence of the football field, sat down fully clothed, and
peed my shorts. Nobody was around. Open space and a bright blue, cloud-dappled sky
seemed to be sweeping me up, as if I were of their same removed and airy substance. I
was floating.

For a while, I sat there with the space and clouds, since movement seemed contrary
to the occasion. After some time, I poured a full bottle of water over my head, stood up

drenched, limped home, showered, and then spent the rest of the day near the toilet.

Feelings? I really don't remember much of anything.

Opening the Floodgates

Bladder incontinence—I'll call it what it is—is a reality for most people with multiple sclerosis (if they say they don't have a problem, they might still be sitting in a field some-where, considering the clouds). It's an early-stage condition of disease progression. Even when I was still running several miles at once, if I had to "go" and couldn't unlock my house door in time, I peed my pants—or at least had some pretty heavy "spillover." Incontinence was my first clue that MS might make my life a little bit challenging. I was horrified.

If I look at what's going on physiologically, my incontinence makes perfect sense. However, scientific explanations don't comfort me much when I'm flying, have to pee, and the turbulence is so bad that not only is the "Fasten Seatbelt" sign on, but flight attendants have strapped themselves to their own fold-down sitters. And science didn't help the flashlight guard or me to blush any less when a random bag search at the Indigo Girls concert uncovered my one extra pair of underwear and my one emergency incon-tinence pad (the only two items in my simple tote).

Science doesn't comfort me in the social arena. I know that most people think incon-tinence is appalling. Horrifying! Disgusting! Can't you control yourself? some might think. Kids joke about it. I used to joke about it. But now that it's my body's reality, I have to face how the condition might revolt people, while not letting it diminish my own confidence in my worth.

Multiple sclerosis is a disease that damages nerves and disrupts impulses, including those running toward my bladder. My brain, like every other brain, sends the message to my bladder and to the rest of my body that I have to pee. The purpose of this impulse is to let the bladder know what might be coming and to mobilize the whole body to seek out a toilet—easy enough communication in a smoothly running body.

When most healthy people send the message their bodies respond with, "Duly noted," and they can breathe and hold it as they search for an outlet. Not so for people with MS. Oftentimes, the message gets sent, the nerve path to the bladder is disrupted, it can't be stopped, it can't be stopped, where's the bathroom? I can't hold it, maybe if I squatted here with my calf jammed up my crotch, it would help to hold it in and nobody would suspect anything, and I wouldn't have an accident right here with all these normal people who can control their pee . . . can't they?

Because I can't expect to hold it efficiently, wide-eyed and breathless, I play mind games to avoid sending and receiving impulses at all. I flat out deny to myself that I have to pee. My bladder might send a message to my brain that it needs something, but my brain pretends it doesn't hear anything about it. It might move my legs to the general vicinity of a bathroom, but we're only really strolling nonchalantly. And, oh, here we are at a public restroom. Maybe I'll just duck in to see if a stall is open. If not, no big deal, because I wasn't really counting on this anyway. Hmm . . . maybe I'll just wait here in line—squatting on my calf!

Silly mind distractions aside, a focus on my bladder has become a sort of awareness practice for me. Without resorting to "flow" charts, I calculate liquid to time to drug to pad ratios with desperate precision. What's the quality and quantity of the liquid I imbibe? Vodka is the least irritating alcohol to the bladder. Where's the next bathroom, how much time will it take me to get there, and might I have to wait in line? Where am I in my menstrual cycle? Are there incontinence drugs in my system, and will they even work considering the quality of the liquid? Oh shit, did I remember to wear a pad? Do I have an extra one?

My bladder also compels awareness since urinating demands of me an attentive biofeedback practice. Simply put, I can't pee when I'm angry. For example, I hardly ever remember to pee first before I get furious with Mike. I might be really pissed-off, "tell him how it is," turn my back on him and storm-limp away as exclamation, stop off at the bathroom because my bladder happens to be *really* full at that exact moment, slam the door after entering, sit on the toilet . . . but I can't do it. Nothing. So I get even madder that he has done this to me, thinking that he must be laughing at my pain . . . but nothing. I might sit there for a while and take the stationary opportunity to play the whole shitty sequence over and over in my head, not to mention what he did to me that other time, and seven years before, and . . . and . . . and . . . nothing. And then I have no choice but to make amends with Mike right there, perched on the toilet, so that my body can get on with its work so I can PEE! I begin breathing in and out deeply, sinking my mind into my bladder until attention mobilizes it again. I call the discipline my "Zen Toilet Ritual," a concept that made a passing urologist laugh heartily.

I and other MSers are not alone, not the only people with an impetuous bladder. Unfortunately, I didn't realize this until I started talking more openly about my own experience. This reminds me of how Audre Lorde never went into hiding with her mastectomy in order to always be seen and recognized by others with the same bodily situation, thus encouraging communication and communion (*The Cancer Journals*). Incontinence is not just a symptom of infancy and old age. New mothers are incontinent, many old mothers are still incontinent, people with other diseases or physical problems are incontinent, some are incontinent when they cough or sneeze, some when they laugh, and some people are just plain incontinent because that's the way they're wired—or isn't wiring *my* problem?

Interesting, though, that despite all the incontinent people out there, I'm always alone in the incontinence pad section of any drug store . . . anywhere. There are ones for every level of "leakage," which if I'm positive enough about the situation, makes me feel seen. Right now, I just need the ones that look like a thick Always pad. I've tried different absorbencies and brands. I prefer Poise Ultra Plus. I swear by Poise! Even though others are cheaper, you don't want to go with an off brand when it comes to peace of mind. The elastic cup is essential.

Knowing now that there are so many incontinent people who aren't buying pads—overtly anyway—I assume that they use drugs. Detrol is wonderful! It completely takes away my urge to pee. However, it also wipes out my ability to urinate at all, which is quite uncomfortable after enough hours. Just guessing that I might need to build up the drug in my system, I start taking Detrol three days before an important event in which I won't have complete bathroom control. Four milligrams is the usual, prescribed dosage, but I take two, in order to balance security with an ability to still "void" without too much discomfort. I have to tell MS friends about the two-milligram alternative since many neurologists know incontinence only by theory.

Incontinence is already a social reality. It happens! But is it too much to hope that it becomes socially acceptable?

Urination in Tanzania is very social. I saw long-skirted women there flare their clothing around them for privacy as they squatted in public. How easy to be incontinent in Africa! How hard to be incontinent in America—but not impossible. My responsibility for change, I think, requires something as simple and as daunting as radical acceptance of my whole body. In living my wholeness, in grounding myself as an entire body—leaky bladder and all. I hope others will see me differently and will think differently of themselves.

Sexy

Living as an integrated body naturally brings up sexiness. Succinctly, can I be both sexy and incontinent? Does one exclude the other? If sexiness is about a presence of body that attracts other bodies, the two realities can most definitely coexist. I'm confident about how my body occupies space—even when I wear an incontinence pad! I'm confident in what I say—even when I'm wearing an incontinence pad! I'm confident in my thoughts, in my knowledge, and in my dreams—even when I wear an incontinence pad! Others listen to me, want to learn from me, and want to connect with me.

MS has forced me to feel and to live as a body more honestly now that I can't control it like I thought I could. Therefore, according to my understanding, I'm sexier in part because I'm incontinent.

My relationship with Mike is a wonderful test of how fully and sexily I live as a body. I realize that after eleven years of marriage, there isn't much room for disillusionment, but I still blush when Mike plucks a Poise pad from the clean clothes, at which point I might whisper in my coy voice, "Do I make you horny?" I do. I know it. It's all about my presence of body. I just wet myself sometimes.

If incontinence is to become a socially acceptable condition, other incontinent people must feel their bodies more intensely also—must feel their sexiness. I facilitated a writing workshop recently for a group of women with MS. Brooke wrote subtly about a recent visit to an urologist who told her to strip but didn't even give her a paper cover-up gown. She felt violated, she said, but didn't share more with us before dropping her stare to her toes.

After she spoke, I eyed the room, considering if it might be the time and place to tell my own story. I felt strongly my will to silence, so I opted for expression. My presence of body—my bladder—demanded it. There among ten women with MS, I recounted the football field story that opened this essay.

When I finished, a dam inside us all seemed to burst open. Valerie, an MS nurse, ran to get incontinence brochures. Movement. I was praised for my ingenious water-bottle cover-up. Smiles. A botanist assured me that the pH of my urine didn't kill the grass. Laughter. The women exchanged incontinence stories and strategies. Releasing the silence opened up a buzz of conversation and created an ambiance of connection, lightness and happiness. The room was breathing again.

I think we were all starting to *feel* our bodies more intensely as we freed our voices to speak our experience. Was it that we were learning to be comfortably sexy in the middle of what we once thought was the greatest apocalypse?

I am incontinent. I have peed on a dishtowel. I have peed in the neighbor's backyard. I have peed beside a mango tree, behind a pine tree, on top of thistle, in a bucket, in white sand, on a boulder, on my own calf, and while holding Mike's hand. I have peed in the Pacific, the Atlantic, the Caribbean, Lake Nicaragua, Lake Powell, the Crystal River, and in a mud puddle. I have peed on the road to Managua, to San Marcos, to Des Moines, to Pella, to Redstone . . . most any road on the way to most anywhere. I pee around.

I am incontinent. When I travel, I fearfully dehydrate myself for the whole trip—but not too much, because that makes me have to "go" too. While I pee, I turn on water to provoke flow and ram my fist into my gut to help my bladder empty. I always know where the next toilet is. I wear a coat or sweater tied around my waist. I keep an extra pair of underwear in my backpack. I buy packages of sixty incontinence pads. I don't wear a catheter . . . yet.

I can't control my body like I thought I could. I feel my body. This is intense.

This is sexy!

WALK-ING

Be-ing is the verb that says the dimensions of depth in all verbs such as intuiting, reasoning, loving, imagining, making, acting . . . that are always there when one is really living.

mary daly, *gyn/ecology*

I am fascinated by the concept of walking meditation for two reasons. First, I can't walk well—sometimes not at all. What a challenge, then, to attempt an awareness practice that represents a barrier to me in name alone. I theorized that the experience might be profound for me, considering that every shaky step I already take directs my awareness to my feet and legs.

The second reason that walking meditation intrigues me is because I was told not to bother with it. All the Web surfing I did on the topic directs physically challenged people to sit while meditating. The info never lauds the potential awareness breakthrough of attempting it with a bum gait. It told me to remain still. But I don't want to.

With MS, I can only tentatively plan the night before for the next day. If I wake up with a fever—as I often do—I can barely get out of bed, and a trip to the bathroom sends me ping-ponging from wall to wall through my hall of squeaky floors, dodging my dog. She thinks we're playing.

This morning I awake refreshed, but I still have to go through a.m. alertness rituals which include a cup of ice water, a heat sensitivity pill, and green tea. Halfway through the green tea, I'm coherent enough to find my glasses, at which point the world materializes enough for me to embrace it—slowly.

I dress, and although I feel good, out of helpful habit I pick up my left leg with both hands, aim it at the leg hole of my shorts, and drop it through with adept precision. Alert and clothed, I'm ready to meditate. I'm ready to move.

I begin . . .

Even though the Internet suggests stepping out the door to feel my feet rest on the ground for a minute or so, I begin by struggling with putting on my bright blue biking gloves, wrestling my wheelchair out the swiftly-closing-in-my-face front door to my too-small-for-both-of-us front porch, and throwing my 20 lb. roller down my railless, concrete steps, across the aggravatingly lumpy grass, down the insufferably chaotic driveway, and to the grassy, concrete sidewalk that runs in front of our tiny home.

Once I get to the sidewalk, I stand upright and breathe, planning to *really* begin the meditation at this point, even though I remember that one major "rule" of walking meditation is to make the practice my own. Tomorrow, I think, maybe I won't cuss at my wheelchair.

Two women are coming my direction, so I pretend to be inspecting my wheelchair tire as they pass. No time to be friendly, I think. I'm meditating!

Pushing my chair slowly down the sidewalk, I breathe and think about my feet first. My sock is all bunched up with my left foot, the one with the new brace that is a bit uncomfortable on my ankle, but not enough to stop me, and the doctor says I'll get used to it, in time, always in time, but doesn't my body fall apart even more in time? Chronic. Progressive.

Exhale . . .

I feel my feet lift and set down, and I try to be intentional about walking in a straight line which the brace helps on account of the plastic sole not letting my foot drop and drag. Two years ago I asked Mike if he noticed that my gait was a little odd, a little shaky. He smiled.

I like what I am doing with my feet, like feeling them, so I relax them and move up my leg to feel clothing and wind on my shins, then knees, then thighs. I am attentive to how they are all working, relax them one by one, and then move up to my hips and pelvis. The sidewalk no longer has grass in the cracks but instead large cement filler nodes in each—like keloids. My wheelchair goes up and down them every couple of steps. I like the roughness. I feel it moving my whole body.

The how-to sheets for walking meditation talk of imagining that my pelvis is carving a three-dimensional triangle as I move down a path. This imagery is fun, but I'm swaying terribly, which frustrates me at first, until I imagine how interesting my triangle must be.

I go around a smooth sidewalk next to a hilly pond and park area. My muscles work differently as I go uphill. My back, neck, arms, all tight. I relax them and re-relax my legs. I feel like a rag doll, and wonder that I am still moving so easily.

I circle the pond, but when I go downhill, my chair wants to run away with my body. I take control again with attention to my legs, arms, back. At the bottom of the hill, I need to rest. I push my wheelchair to the grass and collapse into it. My body feels warm and tingly.

Four ducks float in the pond, move a little, dive a little, bob some more. Their legs must feel good hanging through the cool water. I feel the breeze on mine. I breathe deeply. My eyes close.

But I hear voices! Distant? No, near. My eyes startle open and dart around and around like tracking lasers, like desperation. Do they see me? What do they think? Do they know I'm meditating? They probably think I'm praying—like I just came from church. But I'm not dressed the part.

Inhale . . . exhale . . . inhale . . . exhale . . . I feel my eyes in my head again and forget what came before this breathing.

Do I roll myself home? I enjoy walking. I exhale and stand. I relax my muscles. The birds.

I begin . . .

The breeze on my legs and across my face. I feel cool. The sidewalk cracks. "Bump, bump." "Bump, bump." Happy. Content. "Bump, bump." "Bump, bump." Wheelchair bars in my hands. Waving to a passing car.

"Chook chook." "Chook chook." Old woman in a nightie. Alone. Cutting a hedge. She doesn't look up. I pass, solitary. "Chook chook." "Chook chook."

Shadows. Birds. Leaves moving. Wheelchair up the driveway. Gravel. Crunching sound at my feet. Muscles shifting. Backyard. Park. Sit. Movement of light. Feel it.

Breathe . . .

The following are ruminations about birth and death. Please come join me.

Birth Story

At 1:35 a.m. my water burst as I was drifting off to sleep amid my lumpy but precisely arranged terrain of five pillows. Our evening ended late because we watched a couple Netflix episodes of *24* after a large co-ed potluck baby shower at Kate Bearce's, a shower with about 45 Pella friends, a shower where some said I was ready, but where our friend Lisa insisted, "You don't look miserable enough to have the baby any time soon."

At 1:35 a.m. my water burst. I felt a fleeting, popping sort of pressure inside, wondering if it was just the usual baby head butt to the bladder. But this felt different. I exclaimed, "Oh!" and knew exactly what had happened. The previous night Mike had put a shower curtain beneath the sheet—just in case (we didn't want to ruin our new memory foam mattress, our first baby preparation purchase). Only ten percent of women actually have water break in a gush. I was not a "trickler." I'm not one to beat the odds in disease or in pregnancy.

At 1:35 a.m. I exclaimed, "Oh!" Mike, also newly in bed, questioned, "What?" "My water broke," I said, matter-of-factly. Mike jumped up and began digging under me. "No it didn't," he decreed, finding no wetness, having proven perhaps what he wanted to. He wasn't ready. He had a deadline—needed one more day for getting grades finished for a summer class he had taught. "Yes it did," I said. "My incontinence pad caught it." Sure enough. It was saturated.

Shortly after 1:35 a.m. on October second, 2005, I don't remember what Mike and I said to one another, but I'm sure we were both in a haze, dizzied. We probably playfully cussed a little: "Damn!" "Shit, Nub!" "Holy Crap!" "We have to go to the hospital now," I said. "Why now?" After six weeks of prenatal classes we both knew that broken water didn't mean an immediate trip to the hospital. "Dr. Vande Zande told us to go if my water broke—because I'm so far along already." Even if he had originally estimated October 20th as the due date. I was, in fact, as of the previous Tuesday, three centimeters dilated and fifty percent effaced. How nice to officially, obstetrically speaking, be in labor for a few days and not even feel differently.

Mike and I were slow to move. I thought I felt what might be a contraction—some cramps in my lower abdomen—but the pangs weren't enough to make me rush. I knew, however, that I would be having a baby soon, and maybe that was so surreal that I was impelled to move slowly, meditatively, in the spirit of dreaming.

I hadn't really packed yet for the hospital. I had begun to throw odds and ends into a pile atop a green duffel, but I thought we still had time. Mike, of course, hadn't prepared anything of his own.

I moved the items I stacked on the duffel into the inside: tee shirts, old and new underwear, sweats, two ankle braces, my Lowa boot-shoes, basic toiletries, Sears' *The Baby Book,* our digital camera, a *Sun* magazine, a pillow, and various odds and ends I don't recall, but that filled the duffel. And strangest of all to me, I packed a baby outfit from the Rewers (green velour bootie pants and a greenish onesie). I couldn't believe that we'd be filling the tiny clothing.

I took some time to primp, at least brushing my teeth and combing my hair. I already had freshly shaven legs, and it was a relief not to trouble myself with them. In my months of pregnancy Mike would tease that I shaved only for Dr. Vande Zande and not him. Now he laughs that I gussied up for people I would later poop on.

At 2:15 a.m., 45 minutes after my water burst, we were packed and ready to roll—literally. Sitting in my manual wheelchair and piled with my big green duffel, Mike pushed me to the hospital. The two Pella blocks were quiet and, despite the rut that almost threw me from my seat, our trip was serene. It felt sneaky. I felt both small and larger than life. I was in a wheelchair, but I was powerful. I would be delivering a child. Weren't we, expectant movement and silence, somehow the center of the universe?

Mike and I didn't even know the gender of the baby. We had chosen not to have the ultrasound that would reveal to us the objective sexual parts. "Don't forget," Tim said, "the baby could be a hermaphrodite." Plenty of people in our life made non-scientific predictions. A dangling ring over my belly predicted that I would have a girl. Eriko, who predicted correctly five for five babies also guessed a girl. Our baby doctor declared that if he was a betting man he would say with utmost certainty that the baby will be a girl. Mike said, "No. No. He said the baby might be a boy." My own dreams told me either I would have a two-year-old girl with a bob haircut or a boy who looked a lot like Mike.

On the clear and mild night, while rolling to the hospital to deliver my child, my contractions grew harsher. I timed them as best I could, and I told the nurse who greeted us at the OB ward that I thought . . . wasn't sure . . . but maybe they were four minutes apart and lasting about 25ish seconds.

She directed us into a little examining space, announcing that all six birthing rooms were already occupied, and planning to check me out before making a move to another area. And so I stripped—can't remember what I was wearing, apart from fluffy powder-blue and frog-emblemed slippers that said, "Toadally Cool." (Mike had purchased them for the hospital stay.)

The nurse dug around and found me to be six centimeters dilated. When she left the room to call Dr. Vande Zande, Mike and I kidded around lightly between the harsh pains that popped up to make me wince, pains even harder and closer together than only a few minutes earlier. I tried to remind myself to breathe, which seemed to help, and to call the sensations "contractions" rather than "pains." But at this point the theoretical, all the ideas and ideals about birth and my body, were brushed away like nuisances by a single sharp jab.

And the pangs were stacking up even closer together by the time the nurse returned to say that Dr. Vande Zande would wait at home a while longer until I was farther along. Seeing my discomfort, she dug around for dilation again, sounded surprised as she declared, "Nine centimeters," and hurried into the hall. Mike and I could hear her fluster as she stopped another nurse. "We need to get her into a room," she said. "She's ready!"

Time and space were irrelevant as I became a body in pain. Did pain purify my experience, hone my awareness? I didn't think about it then, but I am sure now that pain must be an escalated path toward enlightenment. I might even say that I have never known myself so thoroughly as when I was feeling my body so concretely and honestly. I had no time then for trite thoughts and sentimental birth "fluff." I, my body, all that I felt and knew, a unity of inside and outside, had become my own mantra.

Inhale . . .

As I stayed with my body, I moved on a rolling bed from the examining room to a vacant Caesarean room, not even lamenting having to miss out on the cozy and "elegant" birthing centers. The room had cold-colored paint and was splashed with fluorescent lights. Sterile. Had I seen it before, I would have hated it. But what was fluorescent light to me when my stomach and thighs were leaping and ripping themselves from the rest of my body?

Exhale . . .

I was transferred to a bed. Uncomfortable. So uncomfortable. I didn't want drugs, but I was, genuinely, surprised by the pain. I understood some women's need for drugs. I understood women. I understood them, but I wanted my pain, as if it were my only comfort. I even waived off the epidural.

Breathe . . .

Lots of movement around me then, people in and out, wearing scrubs, busy and smiling, saying courteous and businesslike things to Mike and maybe even to me. The fetal heart monitor.

The baby is doing well . . .

I talked sometimes, probably nervously and too casually for the occasion, probably about how my thighs hurt, *really* hurt. Ouch! But my words were fleeting and cut off by contractions strong enough to interrupt my affectations.

Breathe . . .

Dr. Vande Zande arrives. I see him down by my left foot, in scrubs and a mask, looking tired, distant and blurring into the cold room. Mike is at my right leg and holding it in his hands. Valerie has my left. I'm sitting up and there are stirrups below my dangling feet. I'm pushing . . .

Long exhale, deep inhale, push, hold breath, "1, 2, 3, 4, 5, 6 . . . 7, 8, 9, 10."

Too long. Ten seconds is too long to push, but I don't say anything.

My thighs are killing me, and so I ask Mike and Valerie to stretch them out between contractions. It feels so good. I breathe.

The baby is doing well . . .

Mike is holding my right leg, and I get frustrated with him as he bends my head too far forward during counting. I hear him: "1, 2, 3, 4, 5, 6, 7, 8, 9, 10."

Breathe . . .

I smell poop and know what I'm doing. The nurses mobilize to clean the area. I looked at Mike. I'm embarrassed. Did I apologize?

The baby is doing well . . .

During some pushes Dr. Vande Zande does something to hurt me down there. Stop, idiot, I'm thinking. He *suggests* I get angry at his fingers. I yell and want to smack *him*, and not just his fingers. I learn later that he was trying to stretch out my perineum.

The baby is doing well . . .

Everybody is slow to count once contractions hit, and so I, frustrated, start without them as they talk among themselves. They catch up with me.

Long exhale, deep inhale, push, hold breath, "1, 2, 3, 4, 5, 6 . . . 7, 8, 9, 10."

Dr. Vande Zande stops the leg stretching between contractions since the motion is pushing the emerging baby back into the birth canal. He worries that I'm fatiguing. "Lift your hips in the air as you push," he says.

The baby is doing well.

He announces that he wants to do a slight episiotomy. "You need a little help," he says. I think I see blurry scissors raised by a cold, distant, faceless figure and nod my head. I think I hear a snip but only feel my thighs aching.

Breathe . . .

My pushing causes more excitement. Still good pushes and ineffective pushes. Still a crowning and then disappearing baby. Still the fluorescent lights and my thighs. Still Mike is holding my right leg.

Still, the baby is doing well . . .

"You're close."

"I'm close?"

"Do you want to reach down and touch its head?"

"Yes." It feels spongy. Hair. I'm brave. My thighs!

Long exhale, deep inhale, push, hold breath, "1, 2, 3, 4, 5, 6 . . . 7, 8, 9, 10."

"It's a boy!" "A boy?" Wet, warm boy on my stomach—to the right. I reach down a hand and stroke the wet, warm boy on my tummy. Sweet words of some sort stretch from me to the wet, warm movement. My boy. My boy? A boy? Mike. I want to hold him, move him to my breast. They take him away to nearby. He's taken away . . . and I protest inside . . . and wait for his return . . . and breathe.

The baby is doing well . . .

At 1:35 a.m. my water burst. Three hours later, at 4:47 a.m. on Sunday, October 2, 2005, our son was born, weighing in at six pounds nine ounces and measuring nineteen inches. He was a healthy pink, apart from the slightly blue feet and hands. Neither Mike nor I cried, which surprises me considering all that we had been through and all that would come.

I'm sitting here now in Marco's second month, watching him sleep and gurgle grunt in his car seat on the couch, finally taking this time to remember backward; but in this retrospect, continually jumping forward also, entertaining fantasies and sometimes fears, crying when a boy is mentioned in a song or on the radio. The result of this sort of consciousness is a Marco maelstrom. Must my—his—birth story be linear?

Mom calls Marco a "miracle baby," referring to the quick pregnancy and healthy baby's arrival, despite all the drugs and their effects: the ten years of birth control, the interferons, the chemo, the couple months of perimenopause. Despite the progressive multiple sclerosis. I also consider him a miracle, but don't look outside and above for a beneficent life/gift-giver. My body is the miracle. My body that is numb and atrophying.

WEANING

Marco didn't want to wean, and I didn't want to wean him, but I did so very slowly and gently, in order to go back on medication I had stopped taking because it was not compatible with breastfeeding. I wrote the following two entries in my journal during the heartbreaking process.

July 4, 2007

Hands aren't working well—better since [I started taking] 4AP, but poorly enough to dissuade me from writing much.

I'm still trying to write about the weaning, which is fully accomplished but really hard for me. I find myself looking for instances of Marco caring about me. Just when I think he has lost interest in me, he'll make a point to hug and kiss me. It feels so good, and I feel needy.

A few nights ago he went to sleep without holding onto my breast. Since then Daddy can put him to sleep or down for a nap. I should welcome the freedom, but it's hard for me. Instead of getting on with my life, I'm a bit lost. Since being in a wheelchair I have been all about Marco. He doesn't need me like before. I knew this time would come, but now what? Get on with my life? I'm more disabled now than I was before Marco.

What does getting on look like for me?

I'm going to try to get my thesis published. That's getting on. But, as far as writing goes, my hands really suck. They're weak. This scares me.

I keep feeling that dealing with disease is what I do. I'm doing a pretty good job, but I can do better. Now with Marco weaned, I'm faced with myself even more. I'm faced with the loneliness of disease even more.

So this is where weaning takes me: I live with disease, and I continue to try to live well. What does it mean?

Well, I still need to say goodbye to breastfeeding. My breasts are drying up. A stage of life is coming to an end. The pain in my breasts is ebbing. I'm sad for that. I'll write my goodbye when my hands work.

July 9, 2007

I'm really sad. I'm so sad that I can't walk with Marco. I can't go to the park, I have to sit under an umbrella at the pool. I go to the pool and am mesmerized by all the mothers sitting and playing with their kids. I miss Marco. When I took away the breastfeeding, I feel like I took away a vital way in which I can be Mommy.

I find myself looking for proof that I'm still important to him. I hate that I do that. Why can't I just be secure? Weaning took away a vital part of my Mommy identity.

Marco is so into Daddy right now, and I really love that. But I wish I could do a tidbit of what Daddy does. I never dreamed that I'd be this sort of mother. I wanted at least three children. It's a wonder that I have held it together. It's a wonder that I'm not depressed. I don't even know how to be close. I love Marco so much.

I find myself dreaming of walking. If I could walk like I did before pregnancy, I could be something of the kind of mommy I had imagined. I do my best right now, but it makes me so sad.

I'll try going swimming with him soon. I haven't because he is mostly in the wading part of the pool. I realized today, though, that the wading area gets deeper. I'll get in.

I'll keep going.

We had a special night a couple nights ago. He woke up a couple times during the night, and I snuggled him to sleep, letting him hold my nipple. We spent most of the night like this. In the morning he sat up and tried to lift up my shirt. As he tried to look under it, he said, "All gone?"

I guessed what he might have meant. "Yes, lovie, leche went bye bye," I said. I thought it was a vital time for us. A couple weeks ago, uncomfortable with not being upfront with him about weaning, not sure what he was understanding, I said to him, "It really hurts Mommy not to give you leche. You know I love you so much, though."

Funny, after our special night of cuddling, he has seemed more distant. I'm not PMS. I was for much of weaning, and so I kept reminding myself not to take his anger and sadness personally. I felt like I was very present for him. I don't feel so present now. I still have to figure out how to be a new Mommy. My love hasn't waned. It will guide me through this new terrain.

Leche all gone

Cyndi

While writing this book, I've been thinking a lot about the women I photographed for my *Bodies in Focus* project. Two women who went through physical transformation because of illness have been on my mind most often. I learned recently that Cyndi had died of pancreatic cancer. I wrote about her portrait, thinking that I might eventually have more distance from her reality. My own words silenced me so much that I could not continue writing. I realized then and still do now, that I do not have distance from Cyndi's reality. According to the bigwig doctors in my life, I am close to death.

I have a hard time believing that Cyndi has passed away, seemingly quickly. If I were to pass away soon, I might kick and scream. This is too soon. I still have things to do.

At the time I met Cyndi, I wondered about her health. Was she at peace? Her urgency to write about her family was so obvious to us in our small group. Did she before she died?

I also feel a sense of urgency to know about the end of Cyndi's life, to know answers to questions that can't be answered now.

Caryn

I've been thinking as well about Caryn, who underwent a mastectomy during her cancer treatment. From Caryn's reflections on her portrait:

"As I breathe in my body, I am so much more aware of how anything can happen. In that anythingness, there's so much room to get lost, and also so much to find."

My response to Caryn's words:

I really like your last sentence. "As I breathe in my body," I am very in touch with things I have lost, but not so in touch with what I've found. I feel like I've lost my relationship with my son, Marco. I'm not nearly the kind of mother I always imagined I'd be. For example, I can't physically play with him, like I had always valued. When it comes to balls, I can't throw them, even slightly. We can't play catch with a baseball, or go to a basketball hoop. I hoped to share with him all the magic that I experienced. For example what did woods mean to me? They are essential to my life. Presently, I can't hike with Marco.

What I have found is hugely important. It is friends. The dictionary tells me that it is akin to French's *mon ami*. It can be translated as my dear friend. I imagine that the word friend is a protector of spirit/soul. In other words it is a protector of being. I feel that friends have enabled my well-being. I am eternally thankful.

As a result of multiple sclerosis health problems, I had to move into hospice in January 2011. The passages below reflect my memories from my first week there. I have written them in the format of e-mail correspondence.

Day 1, Thursday
I came here without thinking that hospice really had much to do with dying.

I plan to write in this journal as I have the chance. I will share my first week here. I write only truth:

I recently brainstormed a list to leave for Marco when I pass away. It lists all of the things that have been most important to me throughout my life. I'll leave it here in snippets:

Reading and Writing
Reading and writing make me feel more alive.

I love to read. I love to write. I know that I am not alone.

"We read to know we're not alone."
- c.s. lewis

I long to journal write. More than writing in order to remember, I write to consider what I think and feel. Only when I am more fully interacting with the world, do I move with power and wisdom.

I was reasonably healthy before multiple sclerosis separated me from my family. Hospice will keep you for a while, I understood. Just until a new care facility has an opening in Pella.

This assumption that going away from home was only temporary proves that I really don't accept the direness of my situation. I am not like most people my age. I am not like most other wives and mothers. I can't escape with Mike to a Caribbean island or to somewhere warm for a golf vacation. I can't float on noodles with Marco over to a poolside refreshment kiosk for smoothies with umbrellas.

Playing the head disconnection game of "I would be" will only let me fly in the clouds temporarily before I realize they aren't as cushy as they appear, and I would eventually fall through and bonk my head as I crash up against reality. Mike and I will never take a vacation together. Marco and I will never float on noodles. Surreal.

Barb comes by to welcome us. She checks in the new patients with questions regarding name, birth date, and funeral home of choice. Mike and I look at one another in disbelief because we had never considered the question. "We haven't really thought about it yet," I said slowly and ethereally, as if speaking from *The Twilight Zone*. "That's okay," she said, crossing off a necessary question. "Just be thinking about it."

When I arrive five other rooms are occupied. We are full. I get there in the afternoon. I smell the cookies baking. Comfort House, they call it. Comfort for the ones dying but especially for those grieving. Comfort.

I am "comfortable" when Mike leaves. In front of the faux fireplace he leaves me. With a goodbye kiss he leaves. Mike leaves. All afternoon I sit in one place, never moving, hardly blinking or breathing, unbelieving that I am actually in hospice. Hospice at 42. Alone. All I really want to do is stare at the wall. Without my family. Surreal.

Betty, hunched over in her simple wheelchair and laboring applesauce to her groping lips, is the first patient I see—but only from across the room. All of our rooms are singles. Only family allowed. Death is otherwise private. Betty has no family here, they say. Dropped her off, moved her in, then left. Does she stare at the walls too?

I am reading about Mother Teresa's decades of "darkness." She initially had a very intimate experience with Jesus, so intimate that she heard a voice (Jesus', she thought) that bid start the Missionaries of Charity. Like Jesus, she experienced God in darkness. Like Jesus, she suffered.

Joe loves to watch the eagles. We are hooked up to wireless. Joe doesn't watch TV like the rest of us—the Iowa evening news booming at rock concert decibels—dueling corn reports. He watches an eagle cam. Hard to have much hubbub for us voyeurs, though, when the extent of excitement is watching big Mama eagle resituating herself on the three eggs. So that I don't miss the action, I bookmark the site on my web addresses. I watch too. It's the rhythm of the place.

As the day is dying down a lonely harmonica plays church hymns. Resident? Family member? Soothing, sometimes missing-a-note, music. Comfort. But not the music I want to die to.

Day 2

When I wake up they tell me that a buncha' friends trickled in to visit me earlier. They were turned away because I was sleeping. They find out that I'm in hospice and all assume that dying is imminent. I am much too quick to tell them that I am only temporarily here until I go back home or a care facility opens up for me in Pella. I am not one of "them." I am not dying soon, anyway. Mike talks that it will be soon. I don't say anything, but I feel hurt. I feel very alive.

The nurse walks into my room, wide-eyed. I quickly ask her for tea—my usual request. She looks so harried, like she's busy with something more important than my drink request. She says, "We are really busy now. We just had two deaths. That never happens." She runs out of the room to get ready for two mini-memorial services. I don't ask who. I, also, remain quiet. Surreal.

We are four.

After a good amount of time I hear a harmonica with a clumsy "God Bless America." Alive. Because I have been lifted and deposited into my wheelchair, I wait by the door to watch a mortician wheel away one shrouded body. I just wanted the new experience of seeing death. My friend is similar, only she likes to sit in a moonlit cemetery. "It's not so much a meditation on death, as it is on the transcendence of life." I think they were two "strangers."

My musical choice for death would not be patriotica.

Today I do not stare at the walls. I even go out the door to the kitchen. There is nice light through the windows. I see Betty "cruising" around in her manual wheelchair. I wonder if she can even see anything from her permanently bowed stature.

Angela and Shawn come with Josh, Angela's just-about-a-man son, and Subway for our weekly gabfest. Lunch date in a hospice house.

Today's topic naturally falls to eagle eggs. "Do they get fertilized before or after they're laid?" Shawn asks, completely straight-faced. Angela and I don't know how to respond. Is she serious, we wonder? Neither of us makes fun of the question because we don't know how to treat it. Is she serious?

Our initial disbelief fades into smart-ass banter. "I know," I say. "The male eagle gets hot and bothered around a female eagle. Then he ejaculates and uses his feathers to wipe the "seed" all over the eggs. Eggs are especially porous. Abracadabara! Eaglets."

Eagle ruminations in our usual segue style naturally lead us to birdwatching. Out of a couple seconds of silent reflection on birds and porn and eagle eggs Angela launches a question. "Fertilization? How do birds procreate, anyway?" "Hmm," Shawn is thinking out loud. "Are birdwatchers not nature lovers at all but porn voyeurs? Are they really trying to sneak a peek?"

Josh perks up. "I'll just Google 'bird porn.'" That's a good idea, I'm thinking as Angela herself perks up. "No no no. You better not Google anything related to porn." Josh and the rest of us laugh. "Duh."

Tomorrow I will ask Mike for forgiveness.

I name my new 2011 journal "As I Lay Living." Shouldn't "lay" be "lie"? Or did Faulkner intend "lay" to be active? Should I really be questioning Faulkner's language usage? Maybe I should read the book.

The weather is unseasonably warm. Phil, the chaplain, stops by with fresh coffee from Smokey Row. We sit on my private porch, both not believing that it could be 68° in January. We agree that God is revealed in the dry pre-spring landscape. Coffee with a new friend . . .

I spend the rest of the day getting ready for a book club baby shower. By "getting ready" I mean that I ask my aide to set up seven folding chairs around my room. I plan to stay in bed. I guess all eight of us will be here.

Jane is all aglow. We throw baby presents at her like confetti, like little scraps from a roomful of gushing and doting oneness. Jane's daddy support is sometimes there, often times absent. We hate him for his absence but love Jane and Owen. We gush. We dote. Jane glows.

Welcoming life in solidarity. After all, hospice is a place to celebrate life.

Jean tells me later that we have a new companion—a woman. Her gender is all the information I can ask.

We are five.

Day 3, Saturday

Blood. I am supposed to menstruate next week, but now it's a full gush. Nurses and aides come in to watch me at full throttle. "We've never seen that around here." It seems like I am a sideshow.

The place is buzzing with family sounds. The harmonica is playing church hymn patriotica. I smell cookies baking, Mike and Marco fly a paratrooper in Central Hall with high ceilings. The itty-bitty parachute is a patchwork of lime green and orange mango, scraps that once soared for real.

I once soared also, but I feel grounded. What can it mean to fly now?

LuAnn stops in to say goodbye. She is setting off on a six-week travel adventure to Ecuador. I am happy for her. Fifty with a husband and two at-home daughters. What has my life become? Surreal. I am traveling vicariously these days. It hurts, but I am happy for LuAnn.

Exploration

We will never find until we first get lost.

We can't begin to find ourselves until we spin dizzy enough to
lose ourselves, to lose the old status quo.

I didn't know what I believed until I traveled far enough away
to be able to point behind and say, "not that."

"There's roads and there's roads
And they call, can't you hear it?
Roads of the earth
And roads of the spirit
The best roads of all
Are the ones that aren't certain
One of those is where you'll find me
Till they drop the big curtain…"
- Bruce Cockburn "Child of the Wind"

"Two roads diverged in a wood,
And I, I took the one less traveled by,
And that has made all the difference."
 - Robert Frost

Mike takes me home with him. John and Beth will arrive soon to our house. When I enter the room, they swarm around me. "You look so wonderful!" "What beautiful color you have in your cheeks!" "Rhonda . . ." speaking loudly and slowly, "this is our grandson, Jacob." I feel like I'm ten years old.

When they figure out that I will not be dying in the next five minutes, they pick up their general chitchat. As usual John has brought music to introduce us to. He is a music professor at Iowa and doesn't leave his work too far behind him.

Mike shows them the book of my travels with Tracy around parts of Asia and Africa in 1992. I recently got it in the mail from Shutterfly, after working on it for 14 months. John is bummed that he didn't bring the album of a musician friend with MS who was too weak to play the trombone, so made a composition of playing the singing bowls. "The album is a testimony to the undying creative impulse." "Darn!" "Next time . . ." He stares out the window.

John asks if I interact with the other patients. "No," I say. "I don't know what I think about that," he says, theorizing.

Mike and I leave for "home" when they do. They say they will come again soon. I remind them that I'm only at hospice for a very short time before they move me to a new care facility when a room opens up. We laugh and wave as if our parting is like any other. We drive the five blocks in silence.

Communication

I love, therefore I communicate. I love Mike and Marco, therefore I communicate with them.

Sharing with others thoughts, feelings, and experiences makes me happier.

We will never have a good relationship, unless we are independent enough to be dependent.

I don't support a politician unless she or he respectfully communicates with me, with my country, and with the world.

Sometimes the best form of communication is silence.

Scott holds the front door open for us. Quiet now in the Comfort House at seven o'clock except for the singing. A catatonic woman in a wheelchair is serenaded by a similarly bent man pulled up to face her in his walker with a seat. Mike and I go slowly by. "Why here?" I ask Mike. He shrugs.

The woman has light in her eyes, but she doesn't speak or move. He starts a song I know. "Softly and tenderly Jesus is calling, calling for you and for me . . . come home, come home, you who are weary, come home . . ."

There is a lot of multi-voiced revelry booming from the room next door, the room with the gentleman (all men are gentlemen here) who watches the egg sitter. Joan comes to greet us. I ask her what's going on. "Joe is Skyping his daughter vacationing in Cancun." Joan is obviously enraptured by the lightheartedness of the unique occasion. "You should meet Joe sometime."

Mike leans over to kiss me. "I won't ever be singing to you." I smile and he leaves. Does he remember our time of intimacy? Of passion? I haven't forgotten. Does he know how much I am hurting? I cannot believe that our relationship has come to this. Surreal.

I will tell him tomorrow.

I am still up at 11, but I comfy-up the room to settle in for another couple of hours.

Caffeine has not affected me for five years. Now that the jazz has kicked in again, I'm using it to have a nightlife. Diana has given me some faux candles to complement my faux fireplace. Is the resulting ambience faux too? No matter, I'm enjoying my room faux and all.

Day 4

I am awake by 11. I used to get up at five o'clock to run four miles six days a week. Then I walked four, then three, then one, and then I swam. Now I don't walk and I don't swim. I can't throw things at all. Surreal.

I hear traveling from room to room an accordion and a singer both—one or two?—screeching hymns. I was readying myself for a quirky show to write about in my journal, but the accordion never peeked through my door. It was still playing enthusiastically elsewhere when a harmonica began belting out its own off-key church hymn repertoire. Is this really the music people want to die to? I'm serious. Is it really? What music do I want to die to?

I drink tea. Sitting up in my hospital bed is the farthest I get before Shawna comes in with a smile and my oatmeal—100% pure Quaker Oats with walnuts, sunflower seeds, dried pineapple, no sugar or honey, and a few droplets of soy milk. I always eat alone in my own room, save for the company of my feeder. I ask Shawna to talk because I am busy mining nuts and seeds from my teeth. They tell me I am a choking hazard. Concentrate . . .

We eat alone. We die alone?

I'm still in bed when Steve comes by "armed" with baguette pieces and apple juice. He asked me a couple days ago if I would be interested in taking communion. I said, "Yes." As I was speaking "yes," he was mumbling about giving me time to think about it. I restated, "Yes." He finally heard me and believed me, so Pastor Steve comes smiling today with the mystical body. I feel ready. He prays for me and finishes by holding my hand sweetly.

Is this communion a sorta last rites ritual, I think? Has nine years of friendship evangelism finally coaxed me to the altar?

"The darkness of faith," Mother Teresa calls it. She suffered the lack of consolation until she died. I suffer a lack of consolation still. I pray silently, "I believe. Please help my unbelief. I doubt. Help."

Jean washes my hair today in bed. We tried to do it in the sink yesterday, but the acrobatics wiped me out, and no water even touched my hair. The new hair washer thingy inflated like a mini pool around my stretched-back head. My hair got wet, but Jean struggles to get the contraption to behave and drain. "Next time I'll do it with a wash cloth."

Theresa sweeps into the room and says to Jean, "I need you when you have the chance." I can tell that somebody has died. Urgency in Theresa's voice? Sudden interruption? I don't know. I can just tell. Not even in hospice a week and I'm already reading death cues. Sure enough, I find out later that Betty has passed away.

We are four.

Does Mike love me? He says he does, but I feel so alone. He and Marco visit once, sometimes twice a day. The first day that I go away from home Marco says, "Daddy, who's going to be Mommy in the house now?

Family and Friends
Relationships are key to my happiness, to my thriving.

Important relationships have been my anchor in life, no matter where my exploration has led me. I have felt very safe to risk, knowing that my family and friends are always here if I need help. I have lots of people to catch me when I fall.

Day 5

Do they still really think that I'm dying? Dr. Vande Zande thought so before. Chronic infection, he said. An open heel wound. Trouble swallowing and breathing. Does he still believe it? I'm not like "them." I feel so alive.

The harmonica is buzzing away again. Church hymn patriotica again. The keyboard accompanies a voice—one person or two?—that matches the accordion exuberance. Dueling cheesy hymns again. The musical quirkiness never ends.

Theresa comes in dangling something in front of her nose and smiles at me sheepishly. I know what time it is. I did this two days ago. An every other day schedule has brought me to this time of flashing my butt hole to the world. Michelle closes the blinds, even though I assure her that nobody can see in when it's light outside. Besides, I say, are there Peeping Toms who hang out at hospice in the daylight?

Bowel Program, that's what they call it. Basically, it means sticking something up my butt so that I can poop. Mike laughs that the medical lingo is so proper, so sterile. You don't "do a bowel program" you "take a shit." You don't "void" you "take a leak."

The harmonica and keyboard both stop. A man's voice rises steadily through the silence. I recognize the melody. Love song. The old man serenades his unmoving but bright-eyed wife. I can't see them from my bed, but their image, tender unto death, transcends walls and time. The man ends his private concert with, "Come home. Come home. You who are weary, come home . . ."

I am ready to get up. Theresa and Jean lift me out of bed with the robot grabber thingy that they call "Hoyer Lift," deposit me at my computer, shut my door, and I play Miles Davis on Pandora. Am I a music snob in the corner room, or am I just asserting in my private way that I would rather die to jazz?

Later, I am sitting by the doorway. Mike, all alone, walks by my room on his way to the kitchen to get his usual cookie. I wave to him as he passes. He waves, too. Is he shy? Carol sees us: "You still really love each other." She sees it. I feel it.

Today is the day.

When Mike returns I ask him to sit on the bed in front of me. I take his hands both in mine, I stare into his eyes, planning to never lose the intimate contact. I will speak from the heart. "Forgive me . . ." I begin with the words of contrition and continue to list the horrible ways I have treated him, ways of people at war, not in love till death do we part.

Among other things, I asked for forgiveness for verbally abusing him in ways that I find really shameful now. For forgiveness for ever making him believe that I didn't think him a wonderful man. "You have been an amazing husband and Daddy." Forgiveness . . . Please forgive me.

Mike leaves to get Marco from school. They will return after dinner. I feel happy.

Hubbub. A new patient has arrived from the hospital Long Term Care unit. Another was going to come also, but didn't want to leave the familiarity of nurses and CNAs from the hospital. Dying is not such a hard thing to suffer. Dying alone must be terrifying.

We are five.

Marco bops in again with Mike. We all love the bouncy boy vitality he brings to this place. The room always smiles when he enters.

Sometimes he flies all his toys that Daddy bought him at a unique flying gadgets toy store, specializing in all kinds of super flyers: planes, paratroopers, and manually twirled spinney flier thingies. Sometimes we play *Yahtzee*. Sometimes *I Spy*.

"I spy with my little eye . . . something that rhymes with . . . snow tire." "No tire," Marco guesses quickly. "No, sweetie," I gently instruct, "you have the right idea about how to make a rhyme, but you need two completely new words, one that rhymes with snow and one that rhymes with tire. I was thinking of f-a-u-x fire." I point to my electric fireplace.

"That's too hard." Mike quickly joins the conversation, as if to scold me for being tough on the boy.

"He's bright. I'll use it a couple times. He'll eventually get it." I turn back to Marco. "Sweetie, faux means fake or pretend. Not real."

We're bored. Great time to play golf! Mike has his clubs, and Marco has his kinda kiddy ones. I have my wheelchair. Together we go outside to a nearby field and hit the ball back and forth.

Before I had children, I used to dream about being a mother to at least three and showing them the wonders of the world: streams, mountains, silence, balls, bodies. I never ever dreamed . . . of this sitting and watching. Surreal . . .

We return, well refreshed but a little windblown. Happy. Alive! While we were away, the new patient died. We feel sad that he didn't get to experience the comfort of the Comfort House. No harmonica, accordion, or synthesizer commemorates his life. He is just gone.

We are four.

After a death the place gets even quieter. I do not hear any music for a while until the harmonica begins playing solemn hymns.

I turn to Marco. "Sweetie, I spy something that rhymes with blow wire."

"Faux fire!" He is beaming.

Day 6

Silence this morning is like an augury. The harmonica. It plays hymns. Somberly. Clearly.

"Joe has passed," announces Sue. Joe who watched the eggs. Joe who Skyped his vacationing daughter. Joe whom I would really like but never met.

Joe's family asks Bob to play his harmonica as Joe passes.

Sue tiptoes in again. "That's sad, Sue." I don't cry, but I remember that he added light to the community here.

"Not really." Sue is perky. "Joe couldn't wait to see his wife in heaven."

Three eggs still.

I imagine this stretcher leaving with shrouded Joe, Joe I never met.

We are three.

Before getting out of bed, I finish up another chapter about Mother Teresa's darkness. I put it down and will never pick it up again. I wanted to read about Mother Teresa's years of "now done darkness," to feel better about my own.

The book is a compilation of letters to her spiritual directors. As she sent them, she would write also to beg for their eventual destruction—preferably by burning. I feel really guilty for having begun the book. In a way, it is as if I am reading a most private journal. Sometimes honesty shouldn't be communal.

The writer wanted to emphasize her great humanity and her great faith.

I saw Mother Teresa in Calcutta in 1992. I saw her humanity:

March 27, 1992

I have seen Mother Teresa several times now at Mass or at evening prayers. After the nuns are on their third or fourth repetition of "Holy Mary, Mother of God," I usually lose concentration and watch Mother Teresa. She is really beautiful. She has osteoporosis, so is permanently bowed before God. Bowed on her knees before God during prayers, she looks like the fruit of the spirit incarnate. Love, Joy, Peace, Patience, Kindness, Goodness, Faithfulness, Gentleness, and Self Control are all shining from her ashen face (she obviously hasn't lain out in the sun lately). I watched her say her Rosary and could see that it was hard for her to catch her breath between each line of prayer, and when she finally did, her lips seemed to move faster, as if she were playing catch up. A little cough or stopping to lick her lips would also put her behind. Even though she has been really sick, she seldom misses Mass and prayers. That demonstrates a tremendous amount of strength and devotion because when I am sick I would much rather focus on God and pray from my bed, than get up and do a bunch of sitting and standing and kneeling and standing Catholic aerobics. I did catch her nodding off one day. Her head was falling, falling and just as it was about to hit bottom she caught it and sprang it up again, blinking her eyes big on the recovery. I liked that because it proved her human.

Mother Teresa said that if she ever were a saint she'd be the saint of darkness. Please let me hold your hand.

I get out of bed, since I'm always uncomfortable here. Robin comes in for a chat, stopping by after visiting her husband with Alzheimer's in another care facility. She visits Ray daily.

She knows my pain.

Robin is the retired college librarian and knew a former occupant of my bed. I didn't need to know that. I like to believe that I am the first person in this bed.

She tells me that she is working on a new reading project for Iowa schools based on the conclusion that the books we read throughout our lives seriously impact us.

She promises to come back soon. I remind her that I will only be here . . . until I go back home or to a new facility . . . or . . . she nods her head.

Does she sympathize with me, imagining my losses in motherhood, marriage, and vocation? Does she shake her head in disbelief that anyone could go on with such loss? I shake my head, too, but I go on. Surreal.

Don't be too long, I think as she goes.

I spend the rest of the day at my computer. I send e-mails. I write in my online journal, my connection to myself and the world. I finish composing my list of important things in my life. I do all this with voice recognition software. I can't type, but I still have a voice.

I fall asleep remembering books, my favorite books. When I was five I loved *Yertle the Turtle.* At ten *Watership Down.* Twelve, Steinbeck's *The Pearl.* Fifteen, Steinbeck's *The Grapes of Wrath.* In college, Dostoyevsky's *The Brothers Karamozov.* In my 20s, Thomas Merton. In my early 30s, Albert Camus' *The Plague* and Cormac McCarthy's *Blood Meridian.* In my mid-30s, feminist writing. Presently, Joan Chittister's writing.

I do not fear death. Death does not silence voice.

Day 7

Alive!

One week here and I haven't died. I won't for a while. It isn't possible. If I do, will they really shroud me too? I'm not like "them." Yes, they will wash my dead body then shroud me just like they do to everybody. Will they be sad to see me go?

The husband is singing to his wife again and the harmonica plays again. Consistency. Home sounds. The house will get two more boarders later today. Who will they be? Will I learn about their quirkiness before they die?

Mike sneaks in and grabs me from behind when I'm at the computer. "Nubby!" "Hey Moo! I thought I'd surprise you." "Why are you here so early?" I'm dumbfounded but not sorry that he came without notice. "I thought you would want to see these letters." He pitches them into my lap. "What are they?" He smiles. "They're from the people who found out you're in hospice. Should I read them to you?" He opens a letter already.

All letters were similarly solemn. Words like "sorry," "tragedy," "keep smiling," "faith," and "love." I am touched but not weepy. When Mike finishes I gather them up and present them back to him. "Please take these home and put them in my study." He looks at me sadly.

"This room is your home now, Sweetie."

So Real . . .

THANKFULNESS

Fellow students together with our gurus, our advisers, all made it possible for me to feel on-fire for most of the time I was at Goddard College. I feel indebted to these people for channeling my passion into a thesis that I have later turned into this book.

Thank you, Caryn, for being my muse and for revealing to me the power of words: for example, how they can change me for the good and how others can utilize them to grow and transform.

Thank you, Lise, for being my muse and for the feminist fire that you ignited in me. Under your tutelage I was guided to write well.

Thank you, Ellie, for being my muse and for your wisdom that led me into the understanding of Embodiment. Your encouragement to revisit my lost art of photography was transformational.

Thank you, Erinn Magee, for being my muse. You warned me against drab colors on my walls and through my body.

Thank you to the circle of women who have made my whole book possible.

Thank you to all my editors: Lisa Bass, Laurie Belin, Nina Forsythe, Danielette Harmon, Paula Henderson (Mom), Robin Martin, Caryn Mirriam-Goldberg, Lise Weil, and Robert Allen.

Thank you, Mat Kelly, for designing my front cover and "Circle of Women" logo.

Thank you, Marco, for being my tie to life.

And thank you, Mike, for the constant hand holding. As always, you have lifted my spirits when I'm down and have listened *ad nauseum* to my verbal processing of my whole experience.

For this book I thank you all. Namaste.

WORKS CONSULTED

Adams, Kathleen. *Journal to the Self: 22 Paths to Personal Growth.* New York: Warner Books, 1990.

Beard, Jo Ann. *The Boys of My Youth.* Boston: Little, Brown and Co., 1998.

de Beauvoir, Simone. "Introduction" to *The Second Sex* IN *Twentieth- Century Philosophy.* Eds. Forrest E. Baird and Walter Arnold Kaufmann. New Jersey: Prentice Hall, 2002.

Berger, John. *Ways of Seeing.* London: British Broadcasting Corporation and Penguin Books, 1972.

Berry, Wendell. "Health is Membership" IN *Another Turn of the Crank: Essays.* Washington, DC: Counterpoint, 1995.

Berry, Wendell. "Writer and Region" IN *What Are People For? Essays.* San Francisco: North Point Press, 1990.

Bordo, Susan. *Unbearable Weight: Feminism, Western Culture and the Body.* Berkeley: University of California Press, 1993.

Daly, Mary. *Gyn/Ecology: The Metaethics of Radical Feminism.* Boston: Beacon Press, 1978.

DeSalvo, Louise. *Writing as a Way of Healing: How Telling Our Stories Transforms Our Lives.* Boston: Beacon Press, 2000.

Desautels, Lisa. "Living From the Inside Out" IN *When the Road Turns: Inspirational Stories About People with MS.* Ed. Margot Russell. Deerfield Beach, Fla: Health Communications, 2001.

Driscoll, Frances. *The Rape Poems.* Port Angeles, Wash: Pleasure Boat Studio, 1997.

Epp, Ellie. "Traumatized Thinking." Quotation from a Goddard College workshop led by Epp, 2003-2004.

Farber, Robert. *Classic Farber Nudes: 20 Years of Photography.* New York: Amphoto, 1991.

Frye, Marilyn. "Oppression" IN *The Politics of Reality: Essays in Feminist Theory.* Freedom, Calif: Crossing Press, 1983.

Frye, Marilyn. "To Be and Be Seen: The Politics of Reality" IN *The Politics of Reality: Essays in Feminist Theory.* Freedom, Calif: Crossing Press, 1983.

Garland-Thomson, Rosemarie. "The Politics of Staring: Visual Rhetorics of Disability in Popular Photography" IN *Disability Studies: Enabling the Humanities.* Eds. Sharon L. Snyder, Brenda Jo Brueggemann, and Rosemarie Garland-Thomson. New York: Modern Language Association of America, 2002.

Gilligan, Carol. *The Birth of Pleasure.* New York: Knopf, 2002.

Griffin, Susan. *Woman and Nature: The Roaring Inside Her.* New York: Harper & Row, 1978.

Henderson, Julie. *The Lover Within: Opening to Energy in Sexual Practice.* Barrytown, NY: Station Hill Openings, 1999.

Hoffman, Eva. *Lost in Translation: A Life in a New Language.* New York: Dutton, 1989.

hooks, bell. "Choosing the Margin as a Space of Radical Openness" IN *Yearning: Race, Gender, and Cultural Politics.* Boston: South End Press, 1990.

Hopkins, Gerard Manley. "Carrion Comfort" IN *Poems.* London: Humphrey Milford, 1918. Bartlby.com 1999. www.bartleby.com/122/.

Jhally, Sut. *Dreamworlds II: Desire, Sex, and Power in Music Video.* Northampton, Mass: Media Education Foundation, 1995.

Lorde, Audre. *The Cancer Journals.* San Francisco: Aunt Lute Books, 1997.

Lorde, Audre. "Uses of the Erotic: the Erotic as Power" IN *Sister Outsider.* Freedom, Calif: Crossing Press, 1984.

Mairs, Nancy. *Waist High in the World: A Life Among the Nondisabled.* Boston: Beacon Press, 1996.

McNiff, Shaun. *Art as Medicine: Creating a Therapy of the Imagination.* Boston: Shambhala, 1992.

McWhorter, Ladelle. *Bodies and Pleasures: Foucault and the Politics of Sexual Normalization.* Bloomington, Ind: Indiana University Press, 1999.

Pennebaker, James W. *Opening Up: The Healing Power of Expressing Emotions.* New York: Guilford Press, 1997.

Phillips, Jan. *God is at Eye Level: Photography as a Healing Art.* Wheaton, Ill: Quest Books/Theosophical Publishing House, 2000.

Rich, Adrienne. "Compulsory Heterosexuality and Lesbian Existence" IN *Blood, Bread, and Poetry: Selected Prose 1979-1985*. New York: Norton, 1986.

Rich, Adrienne. *Of Woman Born: Motherhood As Experience and Institution*. New York: Norton, 1986.

Roorbach, Bill. *Writing Life Stories*. Cincinnati, Ohio: Story Press, 1998.

Rosen, Ruth. *The World Split Open: How the Modern Women's Movement Changed America*. New York: Penguin, 2000.

Sartre, Jean-Paul. "No Exit" IN *No Exit and Three Other Plays*. Trans. S. Gilbert. New York: Vintage Books, 1989.

Schneider, Pat. *Writing Alone and With Others*. New York: Oxford University Press, 2003.

Sewall, Laura. *Sight and Sensibility: The Ecopsychology of Perception*. New York: Tarcher/Putnam, 1999.

Silvers, Anita. "Disability" IN *A Companion to Feminist Philosophy*. Ed. Alison M. Jaggar and Iris Marion Young. Malden, Mass: Blackwell, 2000.

Southerland, Joan Iten. "Body of Radiant Knots" IN *Being Bodies: Buddhist Women on the Paradox of Embodiment*. Ed. Lenore Friedman and Susan Moon. Boston: Shambhala, 1997.

Suleri, Sara. *Meatless Days*. Chicago: The University of Chicago Press, 1987.

The Vagina Monologues. By Eve Ensler. Performed by Central College Theatre, Pella, Iowa. Feb. 2003.

Weil, Lise. *Trivia 15*. n.p, n.d.

Wittig, Monique. *Les Guérillères*. Trans. David le Vey. Boston: Beacon Press, 1985.

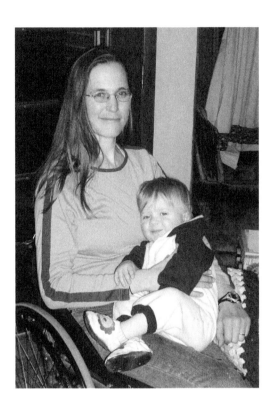

ABOUT THE AUTHOR

Rhonda Patzia is a native of Redstone, Colorado. A professional photographer, she earned a BA in English from Westmont College and an MA in transformative language arts and embodiment studies from Goddard College. At age twenty-two, she backpacked around the world for seven months, journaling and photographing.

Rhonda's photography education began with a couple of courses at Colorado Mountain College and, after travels, with a few courses at Nashville Tech. She has had several photography experiences, which prepared her for the *Bodies in Focus* project in her book, including printing for four years at the Dennis Wile Photography Studio in Nashville, Tennessee. Her photographs have been published in *The Sun Magazine* and have been exhibited in the Fido Coffee House in Nashville, at Goddard College and at the Pella, Iowa, Arts Fest.

Rhonda is currently facility-hopping between Iowa, Colorado, and California.

CPSIA information can be obtained at www.ICGtesting.com
Printed in the USA
LVOW02s0546210114

370294LV00001B/1/P